Binding Testimony

Binding Testimony
Holy Scripture and Tradition

edited by
Theodor Schneider and Wolfhart Pannenberg

on behalf of the Ecumenical Study Group
of Protestant and Catholic Theologians in Germany

Translated by Martha M. Matesich

Bibliographic Information published by the Deutsche Nationalbibliothek
The Deutsche Nationalbibliothek lists this publication
in the Deutsche Nationalbibliografie; detailed bibliographic
data is available in the internet at http://dnb.d-nb.de.

Library of Congress Cataloging-in-Publication Data
Verbindliches Zeugnis. English
Binding testimony : holy scripture and tradition / edited by Theodor Schneider and Wolfhart Pannenberg on behalf of the Ecumenical Study Group of Protestant and Catholic Theologians in Germany ; translated by Martha M. Matesich. — 1 [edition].
pages cm
Includes bibliographical references.
ISBN 978-3-631-65304-3
1. Bible and tradition. 2. Bible—Canon. 3. Tradition (Theology) 4. Bible and Christian union. 5. Christian union. I. Schneider, Theodor, 1930-, editor of compilation. II. Title.
BT89.V4713 2014
220.1—dc23
                                                            2014013261

Cover illustration:
"Verbunden", Beatrix Claßen
Privately owned by Theodor Schneider

ISBN 978-3-631-65304-3 (Print)
E-ISBN 978-3-653-04449-2 (E-Book)
DOI 10.3726/978-3-653-04449-2

© Peter Lang GmbH
Internationaler Verlag der Wissenschaften
Frankfurt am Main 2014
All rights reserved.
Peter Lang Edition is an Imprint of Peter Lang GmbH.

Peter Lang – Frankfurt am Main · Bern · Bruxelles · New York · Oxford · Warszawa · Wien

All parts of this publication are protected by copyright.
Any utilisation outside the strict limits of the copyright law, without the permission of the publisher, is forbidden and liable to prosecution.
This applies in particular to reproductions, translations, microfilming, and storage and processing in electronic retrieval systems.

www.peterlang.com

Contents

Translator's Preface 9

Introduction 11

A. Joint Statement: Canon – Holy Scripture – Tradition 17
   I.   Holy Scripture as the Word of God 17
       1. Our Faith 17
       2. The Understanding of Scripture in the Early Church 18
       3. Our Task 20
   II. The Canon of Holy Scripture: Historical Observations 20
       1. The Genesis of the Canon of the Hebrew Bible 20
       2. The Genesis of the Septuagint Canon 23
       3. The Genesis of the New Testament Canon 24
       4. The History of the Adoption of the Canon 26
       5. Conclusions 31
   III. Fundamental Considerations 33
       1. Ecumenical Convergences 33
       2. The Canonicity of the Canon and Its Justification 37
       3. The Size of the Canon 39
       4. The Problem of Authentic Scriptural Interpretation 41
       5. Frame of Reference for Contemporary Ecumenical
          Teaching on Scripture 42

B. Concluding Report: The Understanding and Use of Scripture 49
   1 Introduction: The Ecumenical Context and Our Objective 49
       1.1 Our Shared Conviction 49
       1.2 The Previous Ecumenical Discussions 50
       1.3 Our Efforts 55
   2 Holy Scripture as the Word of God 57
       2.1 Our Shared Confession 57

	2.2	Divine Inspiration	58
	2.3	God's Word in Human Words	61
3	Worship as the Location Where God's Gospel Is Proclaimed		64
	3.1	The Connection between the Bible and the Liturgy	65
	3.2	The Relationship between Faith and Celebration	66
4	The Unity and Totality of Holy Scripture		68
	4.1	The Task	68
	4.2	The Profession of the Oneness of God and the Unity of Scripture	70
5	The Two Testaments in the One Holy Scripture		72
	5.1	The Significance of the Old Testament	73
	5.2	The Significance of the New Testament	77
	5.3	The Tension-filled Unity of the Old and the New Testament	78
		5.3.1 Models of Interpretation in History	79
		5.3.2 Foundations of a Contemporary, Ecumenical Definition of the Relationship	83
6	The Center of Holy Scripture and the Diversity of Its Theologies		85
	6.1	The Evangelical-Lutheran Tradition	87
	6.2	The Reformed Tradition	91
	6.3	The Roman Catholic Tradition	92
	6.4	The Discussion Today	95
		6.4.1 The Need to Make Distinctions in Keeping with the Gospel	96
		6.4.2 The Discussions concerning a "Canon within the Canon" and a "Center of Scripture"	96
	6.5	Unity through Diversity – Diversity through Unity: An Ecumenical Perspective	97
		6.5.1 The Entire Holy Scripture in Its Orientation towards God and towards Christ	97
		6.5.2 The Unity and Diversity of Scripture – The Unity and Diversity of the Church	98
7	Law and Gospel		99
	7.1	Lutheran Theology	99

		7.2 The "Catholic" Precursors	100
		7.3 The New Testament	101
		7.4 Hermeneutical Significance Today	102
8		The Interpretation of Scripture in the Life of the Church	103
	8.1	The Interpretation of Scripture as a Fundamental Activity of the Church	104
	8.2	The Interpretation of Scripture in the Liturgy	105
		8.2.1 The Use of Scripture in the Liturgy – Fundamental Considerations	106
		8.2.2 The Scripture Reading	108
		8.2.3 The Sermon as Interpretation of Scripture	110
		8.2.4 The Psalms in the Liturgy	111
		8.2.5 Other Old and New Testament Hymns of the Liturgy	112
		8.2.6 Hymns and Songs Based on Biblical Quotations and Motifs	113
		8.2.7 Liturgical Prayer	114
		8.2.8 The Diversity of Scriptural References and the Unity of the Liturgical Witness to Faith	116
	8.3	The Scholarly Interpretation of Scripture in Exegesis and Systematic Theology	116
	8.4	The Significance of the Interpretation of Scripture for Ecumenism	118
		8.4.1 The Development in Protestant Theology and in the Protestant Church	118
		8.4.2 The Development in Roman Catholic Theology and in the Roman Catholic Church	121
		8.4.3 The Ecumenical Significance of the Scholarly Interpretation of Scripture	122
	8.5	The Significance of Scholarly Exegesis for the Church's Interpretation of Scripture	123
		8.5.1 The Doctrine of the Multiple Senses of Scripture	124
		8.5.2 The Search of Exegesis for the Historical Sense of Scripture and the Question concerning the Binding Nature of Scripture	127

	8.5.2.1	The Hermeneutical Approach of Exegesis ..	128
	8.5.2.2	The Theological Significance of Scholarly Exegesis	129
	8.5.2.3	The Tension between Historical and Contemporary Scriptural Interpretation	130
	8.5.2.4	The Task of Scholarly Exegesis in the Service of the Gospel	132

9 The Interpretation of Scripture and the Binding Teaching of the Church 133
  9.1 Our Starting Point and Procedure 133
  9.2 The Biblical Understanding of Doctrine and Teaching Office – A Summary 134
    9.2.1 Doctrine 135
    9.2.2 The Teaching Office 136
  9.3 Holy Scripture as the Sole Criterion for Proclamation and Tradition as the Location for Attaining Certitude 137
    9.3.1 Our Shared Convictions 137
    9.3.2 Denominational Characteristics 141
      9.3.2.1 Protestant Theology 141
      9.3.2.2 Catholic Theology 146
    9.3.3 Conclusions 149
  9.4 The Overall Responsibility of the People of God as Bearers of the Faith Tradition 150
    9.4.1 Our Shared Convictions 150
    9.4.2 Denominational Characteristics 152
    9.4.3 Conclusions 155
  9.5 "Teaching Office of the Church" – the Special Responsibility of Ordained Ministers 155
    9.5.1 Our Shared Convictions 155
    9.5.2 Denominational Characteristics 159
    9.5.3 Conclusions 168
10 Epilogue: God's Spirit in God's Word 171

Translator's Preface

Brief mention should be made of a few points to assist the English readers of the texts published here.

The German word "evangelisch" has, for the most part, been translated as "Protestant". For example, the source of the present volume is the German-speaking "Ecumenical Study Group of Protestant and Catholic Theologians." On the Protestant side this group includes theologians of both the Lutheran and Reformed traditions, but not theologians from other Protestant denominations. In the texts "Protestant" also refers to the German-speaking Reformation tradition of the 16th century and is used as a general description for the positions of the Reformers over against the Roman Catholic tradition. In this sense the text often speaks of "two sides" or "two churches." The term "Protestant" is thus restricted in its use here, and this should be borne in mind.

If the information was available, the bibliographical data for the English translations of German books appear in the footnotes. If it was not possible to obtain the English edition and to provide the page numbers in the English book, the footnote gives the information for the German edition.

The authors of the texts quote different German translations of the Bible. Unless otherwise noted this English edition uses the *New Revised Standard Version* throughout, sometimes abbreviated NRSV.

For Church documents the first reference is to Denzinger-Hünermann, abbreviated DH, which was used in the German texts: H. Denzinger, *Kompendium der Glaubensbekenntnisse und kirchlichen Lehrentscheidungen*, improved, enl., transl. into German and ed. by P. Hünermann in collaboration with H. Hoping, 39th edition, 2001, Freiburg in Breisgau, Basel, Rome, Vienna

1991. The second reference, placed in brackets, is to Neuner-Dupuis, abbreviated ND, if the documents or at least parts of them can also be found there: J. Neuner and J. Dupuis, *The Christian Faith in the Doctrinal Documents of the Catholic Church*, ed. by J. Dupuis, 7th rev. and enl. edition, New York 2001.

The texts of the Second Vatican Council were taken from Walter M. Abbott, gen. ed. and Joseph Gallagher, transl. ed., *The Documents of Vatican II*, New York 1966; the texts of classical Protestant documents were quoted from *The Book of Concord: The Confessions of the Evangelical Lutheran Church*, transl. and ed. by Theodore G. Tappert, Philadelphia 1959.

Any explanations or remarks appearing in brackets [ ] have been added by the translator. In the English edition *errata* found in the German text have been corrected.

I would like to thank Mildred M. Edwards for her skillful and patient editing and her excellent advice and encouragement. I alone am responsible for any remaining errors in the translation.

Martha M. Matesich

Introduction

A Brief Explanation

Theodor Schneider

With the completion of the third volume of papers our project "Binding Testimony" has come to an end for now and the work of the Ecumenical Study Group on the fundamental topic "Sacred Scripture" is finished for the time being.

Our study group devoted itself to the project "Scripture – Tradition – Interpretation of Scripture" in the spring of 1986 following the conclusion and publication of our studies on the condemnations of the Reformation era.[1] The subtitles of the three volumes of "Binding Testimony" now available in our series "Dialogue of the Churches"[2] illustrate that during our twelve years of work we definitely tried to consider the entire range of problems and see it in all its details: *Canon – Scripture – Tradition* (volume 7); *Interpretation of Scripture – Teaching Office – Reception* (volume 9); *The Understanding and Use of Scripture* (volume 10). A closer look at the topics and subject matter of the individual papers and at the compilations of the results in the "Joint Statement" of the first volume and the "Concluding Report" of the third volume, for which we are jointly responsible, reveals that the individual thematic complexes have been presented and discussed in varying detail. That was by no means the original plan. But a gathering of about forty scholars, including the recent addition of some women, which meets once a year for a week-long conference is a living entity. Its opinions and wishes cannot sim-

---

[1] Cf. K. Lehmann and W. Pannenberg, *The Condemnations of the Reformation Era: Do They Still Divide?*, transl. by M. Kohl, Minneapolis 1990.
[2] Cf. W. Pannenberg and Th. Schneider, ed., *Verbindliches Zeugnis I: Kanon – Schrift – Tradition*, Freiburg, Göttingen 1992; *Verbindliches Zeugnis II: Schriftauslegung – Lehramt – Rezeption*, Freiburg, Göttingen 1995; *Verbindliches Zeugnis III. Schriftverständnis und Schriftgebrauch*, Freiburg, Göttingen 1998.

ply be planned and predicted; they are instead influenced by exterior and interior spontaneity and, in no small degree, also by the professional workload of the members. Thus the fact that nearly all the colleagues are kept unduly busy by their assorted involvements in committees and projects in addition to the regular business of the university also made itself felt. Individual specialists in certain subject areas were not always in a position to contribute their knowledge of the subject to the greatest extent possible at every phase of the preparation of a topic which caused some delays. On the other hand it happily turned out that the exceptional expertise of individual members or their special interests as determined by their situations enhanced their tremendous involvement in and contribution to certain thematic sections.

Thus we could present and reassess thoroughly and in detail the history and theology of the biblical canon as well as our shared scriptural understanding of the Bible, the Old and the New Testament. By contrast, the thorny and huge problem of identifying or developing an appropriate, authentic, and binding interpretation of Sacred Scripture caused us considerably more trouble. This was, of course, due above all to the complexity of the matter. Nevertheless, the various papers written over 10 years present and discuss the central themes and concerns of the denominations and their diverse emphases, terminologies and customary ways of speaking.

Our efforts to compile and organize the widely diversified treatment of the controversial points, the settled misunderstandings, the successful clarifications, the newly opened approaches for understanding, and the respective advances in knowledge as well as to merge all this into a precise, sufficiently detailed, yet manageable text spanned a full three years and resulted in the "Concluding Report" printed at the end of the third volume.

After discussing and clarifying the issue that the topic of the "infallibility" of the church and its magisterium, which is of course also connected to the topic of scriptural interpretation, should not be handled within the framework of this project because it needs a thorough treatment of its own in the future, we began our consultations on the content and form of a concluding joint statement at Castle Hirschberg (Beilngries) during the annual conference of 1995. The group, chaired by Eduard Lohse, decided that the text planned for the conclusion should be entitled "The Understanding and Use of Scripture" and that, in addition to an introduction outlining the ecumenical context, it should initially include six thematic sections, namely: *The Essence and Unity of Scripture*; *Law and Gospel*; *The Word of God in Human Words*; *Criteria for Interpretation*; *The Use of Scripture in the Liturgy*; *The Use of Scripture and Doctrinal Decisions*. A number of colleagues volunteered to prepare draft texts for the individual sections.

At the two annual conferences which followed in 1996 (at Castle Friedewald) and in 1997 (at the Catholic Academy of Hamburg) we were thus able to discuss the texts of varying lengths.

In the course of these consultations which spanned several years our experience was similar and the result comparable to what had occurred during the earlier project, "The Condemnations of the Reformation Era." The more specifically and more precisely we viewed, pondered and described the separate issues, the more detailed the written version necessarily became. The outline changed and the length of about 40 pages originally planned in 1995 was more than doubled – but, at least in our opinion, not to the detriment of the achieved clarifications and convergences.

In the spring of 1997 a study group was selected in Hamburg, which produced a master text. This text was sent to all the members with the request that they express their proposed changes in writing. The numerous suggestions for improvement were worked into the text as far as possible so that the "final version" could be sent to all the members for the concluding conference at Castle Friedewald from March 30 to April 2, 1998. During the days of work at that conference further changes were discussed and included before the final vote was taken on April 2, 1998. All the Protestant and Catholic members who were present approved this "Concluding Report" – except for one.

Although the group as a whole felt that the third volume should finally be published, this does not mean that we think our work cannot be improved upon or does not need additions. In the concluding discussions we stressed repeatedly that it would be worthwhile to investigate this or that question even more thoroughly than has hitherto been done. A few colleagues in particular set the whole group thinking with their observation that we had not even tackled the vital and necessary task of actually conveying the central message of the Bible into the language of today, into the situation of our own lives, of crystallizing the "essence of Scripture": God lives and speaks and loves today; God is our God; God's promise is the word of inspiration and liberation precisely in our plight, the saving escape out of our blind alleys. We had moved instead in theological circles, dealing with the traditional problems of theological debate and using the familiar language game of theological specialists. We dashed off arguments and insights, all of which were not entirely new, but had already been thought out and stated previously in their separate elements in this or that form in the relevant publications.

But does anyone really have an overview of the relevant discussion as a whole, or has anyone absorbed it and actualized its results? Both independently and in conversation with each other we discovered again and again that the established theological positions of other church and denomination, and even of the other theological disciplines within one's own denomination, are still unknown and in no sense whatever part of our common heritage. Ah, how we have all become such specialists! Yet, in spite of everything, we are of the following opinion – although with a certain degree of hesitation as an expression of our reservations: Because of the fundamental importance of this joint assessment of the content-related and methodic significance of Sacred Scripture and its living tradition in our time for our common path of faith in the new millennium, we want to present the results of our professional efforts in this area to the ecclesiastical and academic community in the hope that these findings may benefit the dialogue in the broad ecumenical movement of Christianity. At the same time we are grateful for every addition and any work that advances this endeavor.

Volume I of our project "Binding Testimony," published in 1992, includes ten papers by members of our study group which served the mutual exchange of information and functioned as the basis for discussions, as well as a "Joint Statement" which summarizes the initial results of our investigation. Volume II, published in 1995, contains eleven additional essays on the overall topic. In volume III there are once again thirteen relevant papers from the perspectives of the different theological disciplines as well as the "Concluding Report."

The present publication only presents the **results** of our many years of efforts for which we are jointly responsible, namely:

– the "Joint Statement" entitled "Canon – Holy Scripture – Tradition," and
– the "Concluding Report" entitled "The Understanding and Use of Scripture."

Ecumenical Study Group of Protestant and Catholic Theologians

Canon – Holy Scripture – Tradition

Joint Statement

The church lives from the word of God which is given to it in the testimony of Holy Scripture. Despite this conviction shared by all Christians, there have been different views about the scope of Sacred Scripture, about its interpretation, and about the role of the teaching authority of the church which is connected to its interpretation. These differing views have existed since the era of the early church and especially since the Reformation. Many judge these disagreements to be divisive factors.

The following explanations (and the efforts leading up to them) should contribute to clarifying the problems arising from these differences and thus to a greater unity in Christ.

On the basis of the conviction we share with all Christians, our explications concern above all an agreement on the evolution of the canon of biblical books, the ecumenical possibilities opened up as a result of this, and the relationship between Holy Scripture, tradition and the binding teaching of the church.

I. Holy Scripture as the Word of God

1. Our Faith

We Christians believe in the triune God. We hear God's word in the holy scriptures of the Old and the New Testament. These witness authentically to what God says and does.

"Through his word God created the world (Gen 1); He revealed Himself to His people in the Old Testament in the text of the Law and through the prophets (cf. Heb 1:1 f.); He has remade us into His people through his word (1 Pet 1:23–25; James 1:18); His word proclaims the fulfillment of all promises.... The Son, crucified and risen, stands in the center of God's revelation in the word. He Himself is God's Word from all eternity (Jn 1:1; cf. Heb 1:2) and God's Word as a historical person in whom the judging and re-creating work of the triune God reaches its goal. (Jn 1:14; cf. 2 Cor 1:20; Rev 19:11 ff.)....

"Jointly we call Holy Scripture God's word because the witness of the prophets and apostles whom God entrusted with His word is brought together in it in a valid way....

"Talk about Scripture as the word of God is attested in the New Testament itself; it has its origin in the word of God as living proclamation, above all in the proclamation of the gospel (1 Thess 2:13; 2 Pet 1:16–21; cf. 2 Tim 3,13–17). And precisely as such it has proven its power and validity in the history of the church."[3]

Holy Scripture as the word of the triune God through which God authoritatively acts as judge and savior has to be valid in this sense. Scripture has its primary place in the liturgy of the Christian congregation; here it exercises its spiritual influence through which a congregation is assembled, edified and perfected.

2. The Understanding of Scripture in the Early Church

The trusting certitude that the mysterious, living God has "spoken", that He Himself has made and will make Himself discernable to the people and to

---

[3] Bilateral Study Group of the German Bishops' Conference and the United Evangelical-Lutheran Church of Germany, *Kirchengemeinschaft in Wort und Sakrament*, Paderborn, Hannover 1984, pp. 10–12. This document has the basic approval of both church governing bodies: Cf. "Ökumenischer Dialog über *Kirchengemeinschaft in Wort und Sakrament*," in: Arbeitshilfen 59, Bonn 1987.

many individuals is already the foundation of the way Israel understood itself. God's loving attention and demands experienced in particular historical circumstances were articulated in the numerous testimonies of the people affected and assumed various forms that were already expressed in writing very early on. The "Sacred Scripture" or "Holy Book" (2 Mac 8:23) that evolved in this way in a centuries-long process of transmission "documents" the permanently momentous deeds of God and also promises them to all later generations. The first Christians who were part of this tradition and shared this conviction (cf. 2 Tim 3:15–17) formulated their belief in Jesus Christ as the incarnate Word of God by explicitly referring back to the holy texts of Israel since they read and heard these texts as a matter of course from the perspective of Christ and in relation to Christ (cf. Lk 24:25–27,32,44; Acts 8:30–35, 2 Cor 3:14–16), seeing in him God's definitive promise of Himself: "Long ago God spoke to our ancestors in many and various ways by the prophets, but in these last days he has spoken to us by a Son.... He is the reflection of God's glory and the exact imprint of God's very being...." (Heb 1:1–3).

The certitude of those believing in Christ that they had received the decisive illumination for understanding the Holy Scriptures of Israel through the glorified Lord (cf. 2 Cor 3) relegated these texts to a certain "provisional realm," but preserved them at the same time precisely through this designation as "Old Testament," as a witness to the interpretation and fulfillment taking place in Jesus Christ, and thus as the permanently momentous word of God.

Thus the books of the New Testament with the good news of those who proclaim the fulfillment in sermons, epistles and gospels, being inspired by the same God who once spoke through the prophets (cf. 1 Pet 1:10–12), ultimately join those old texts of instruction and promise.

This differentiated, tension-filled outer and inner relationship between Israel's scriptures and the gospel of Jesus Christ remained the fundamental conviction of the Christian church against every challenge and controversy: "There is one God, the Father ... and one Christ, Jesus the Lord, who went through the entire order of salvation and brought everything together in Himself" (Irenaeus, Adv. haer. III, 16.6). The Bible of Christians as a literary work thus includes the Sacred Scriptures of the Old and the New Testament.

3. Our Task

First of all we shall consider in particular the older part, taking seriously the fact that the collection and definitive demarcation of the books of the "Old Testament" represent an independent historical process. This is not only demanded out of respect for Judaism, whose Bible has remained the "Hebrew canon" to this day. It is also and above all required because many times throughout history this canon has lastingly impacted the exact determination of the content of the Christian Bible in such a way that denominationally different lists of the "canonical books" of the Old Testament are still kept today.

This situation confronts us first of all with the task of reaching an ecumenical agreement on the determination of the canon of Holy Scripture. To accomplish this task it is imperative that we take a look at the history of the genesis of the biblical canon.

In part III we then treat fundamental considerations concerning the theological relevance of the formation of the canon and attempt to provide a joint determination of the relationship between "Scripture" and "tradition" in view of this fundamental, early Christian process.

II. The Canon of Holy Scripture: Historical Observations

1. The Genesis of the Canon of the Hebrew Bible

The historical development of the canon of the Hebrew Bible spans a period of half a millennium and takes place in many stages.

1.1 A *prehistory* going back to the period before the exile is evidenced by the fact that certain responsible regional groups compiled and passed on collections of texts which on the one hand were meant to be authoritative, but on the other hand were neither completed yet nor inalterable. Instead, these texts were continually being expanded and interpreted – at least in part precisely because of their abiding claim to validity. In a procedure understood as redaction history different text traditions were joined together, probably after the appearance of Ezra, into a uniform presentation of the shared history of faith, i.e. into the great historical work of Gen 1 to 2 Kings 25.

1.2 Against this background *the first step* in the direction of a canon of sacred texts was taken in the 4th century B.C.E. The Torah, the part containing the laws, was set apart in order to function as the required national law of the province of Judah in the Persian empire. From this point on the Pentateuch acquired universal validity in Judaism as a definitively concluded work (in which the chronological systems at most would still be altered). This canonical "authority for orientation," the Torah, did not, however, preclude in any way people's esteem for the other older texts or for new texts of religious guidance; it entered instead into a varied and fertile relationship with them.

1.3 *The second step* in the growth of the canon of the Hebrew Bible probably occurred during the period of the Ptolemies in the second half of the 3rd century B.C.E. Determined to dissociate itself from the central ideas of Hellenistic culture and lifestyle, an eschatologically attuned segment of Palestinian Judaism, which had an anti-Hellenistic and an anti-Ptolemaic orientation, consolidated the part of the Jewish Bible later called "Nebiim" (Joshua – Malachi) into a collection of texts which, following the example of the Torah, was to be considered from then on as inalterable. In contrast to the Torah it did not achieve canonical recognition in all groups of Judaism – notable exceptions being the Samaritans and Sadducees.

Our notion of "canonical" must also not tempt us here into making a false historical judgment, as if Nebiim and Torah were understood in this period as an "exclusive" conclusion that would have henceforth precluded the formation of other guiding, authoritative texts. Rather the act of fixing texts conclusively by canonizing them and the process of assuring oneself theologically of their content by updating them through the addition of other texts stand in a dialectical, contingent relationship to each other.

1.4 The formation *of the third and last part* of the Hebrew canon was anything but a linear development. In the three centuries until the end of the first century after the birth of Christ a great variety and diversity of theological currents and groups of traditions set the tone. In addition to Qumran and apocalyptical circles, the group made up of a temple-oriented ruling class with wisdom-eschatological characteristics achieved great appeal. It talked about "the other, remaining writings" – in addition to the Torah and Nebiim (cf. Intro. to Sir). Temple-oriented writings of a wisdom-ritualistic nature were gathered in this collection which had not been entirely completed at the time of Jesus. The Book of Psalms obviously played a special role here as a crystallization point. There is support for the assumption that the canonical validity of the third and last part of the Hebrew canon, the "Ketubim" (Writings), was established in the Pharisaic milieu during the course of the first century after the birth of Christ.

At the end of the first century this determination of the canon was finished, although – as one would expect – a certain flexibility still existed. 4 Ezra 14 [2 Esd 14 in the NRSV], for example, acknowledges 70 other writings for the wise and the theological teachers in addition to the 24 books of the defined canon. By contrast, with his fixed specification of 22 books Flavius Josephus confirmed (*Against Apion* I.39–41) for the last decade of the first century that the tripartite Hebrew canon, as we know it, was definitively delimited and considered to be a self-contained whole. This was justified by means of a kind of "canon theory," namely by the temporal-genetical criterion of a "prophetic succession" which pertained to Mosaic and post-Mosaic prophetic writings from the time of Moses until Ezra (at the time of Artaxerxes I, 465–425 B.C.E.). Politico-religious considerations as well as Judaism's need to dissociate itself from apocalyptic groups who believed the end was indeed imminent certainly played a role in this "Pharisaic" formation of the canon during the catastrophic events near the end of the first century after the birth of Christ. Also playing no small part in this development was the attempt of Pharisaic Judaism to distance itself from the Greek Bible of the diaspora Jews, the so-called Septuagint (LXX), since it was increasingly becoming the Bible of the Christians.

2. The Genesis of the Septuagint Canon

2.1 Work on the translation of the Holy Scripture of Israel for the *Greek-speaking Jews of the diaspora* already began in Alexandria in the first half of the third century B.C.E. The historical background for the information given in the *Letter of Aristeas* concerning the origin of the LXX is the fact that the Torah was translated into Greek under Ptolemy II Philadelphus (284–246). Although the Pentateuch received much greater attention in Alexandria in the following period than the other historical and prophetical writings which were known through a lively exchange with the Palestinian homeland (cf. 2 Macc 2:15; SirProl), their translation into Greek, which in some cases occurred in Palestine, was also completed for the most part by the time of Jesus. Ecclesiastes (Cohelet) and the Song of Songs, however, as well as Ezra and Nehemiah were probably not translated until sometime during the course of the first century after the birth of Christ; in this process parts of older translations were revised on the basis of the original text. It is clear that the Palestinian-scribal influence in particular played a role here. Among other things the scribes wanted to have the more recent writings of the emerging "Hebrew canon" also recognized in the diaspora.

All in all this translation endeavor was a complex process. Occasionally there were several versions for the same book, and some of them had an older text form than the later Masoretic text. At the same time the translators were very free about shortening or adding to the text in some places. This in particular reflects the still relatively open "canonicity" of these writings in the Palestinian homeland. On the other hand, in this way the Greek-speaking diaspora also took an active part in the process of definitively "canonizing" Holy Scripture – albeit under different conditions and with somewhat different interests. Its considerable influence is illustrated in particular by the fact that in Alexandria and other centers of the Jewish diaspora additional religious writings from the Hellenistic-Roman period acquired heightened esteem in their Greek translation as favored "devotional literature," namely the "deuterocanonical" books of Tobit, Judith, Baruch, Wisdom, Ben Sirach (Ecclesiasticus), Maccabees and the additions to Daniel and Esther. The greater part of these texts, however, had originally been written in Hebrew or Aramaic and also bore the imprint of Palestinian Torah-piety.

2.2 The first letter of Clement as well as different early Christian authors up to Tertullian and Clement of Alexandria verify that very early on *the Christian circles* of Rome, Carthage and Alexandria knew of and were impressed by these works and the piety of the Jewish diaspora conveyed in them. The evident popularity of the writings added to the canon of the Hebrew Bible, especially in Western Christianity, is also corroborated by their early translation into Latin (*Vetus Latina*, the beginning of the third century C.E.). Incidentally, it is no longer possible to determine how each one of these books combined with the others to form the Septuagint canon of the "Old Testament" as it is contained in the codices since the fourth century C.E.

3. The Genesis of the New Testament Canon

3.1 The "books of the New Testament" emerged in the service of both proclamation and the formation of the congregations. The Old Testament stood apart from them as "Holy Scripture," which, however, had become an interpreted norm through the preaching of Christ.

3.2 Until the early second century the church was convinced that it still had direct access to the *preaching of the Apostles* which lived on in oral tradition. "The living and enduring word" (Papias) was considered to be a normative authority since the glorified Kyrios speaks and acts in it in his Holy Spirit.

3.3 The recording of the New Testament message and the keeping of individual texts in the congregations, the collection of the letters of Paul and the "four Gospels," and especially the reading of these scriptures in worship can be seen as *first steps towards the formation of a canon*. The works of the Apostolic Fathers show continuous contact with New Testament scriptures. Not all the allusions, however, should be interpreted as quotations from already existing New Testament works. Likewise, an explicit appeal to "the Gospel" must not always be understood as a reference to a written gospel; its primary purpose is first of all to stress the harmony with the original Christian message. But where a saying of the Lord is connected to a known Old Testament saying and described at the same time as *graphé*, one may assume that the special quality of the New Testament scriptures has already been recognized.

3.4 The development during the second century was marked by the *experiences of contradictory interpretations* and conflicting uses of the apostolic kerygma. The coexistence of and antagonism between different expressions of "Christianity" compelled believers to recall their own origins and the normative significance of these. In particular to counter Marcion's radical isolation and restriction of "binding" tradition to the writings of St. Paul and the Gospel of St. Luke, the congregations of the large churches combined what they considered to be gospel, what was familiar to them as apostolic tradition and what they knew was in line with their preaching. This declaration of the agreement of their own preaching with the authentic, original message also applied explicitly to the revelation of the "Old Testament."

3.5 Around 200 the first and *decisive phase of the determination of the scope of the New Testament canon* was concluded. At the end of the second century tables (in the works of Irenaeus, Tertullian, Clement of Alexandria and others, as well as in the "Muratorian Canon") listed those writings from the early period of the church which had been recognized as normative: the four Gospels, the Acts of the Apostles, 13 epistles of Paul, Hebrews, Jude, 1 Peter, the epistles of John and the Apocalypse. The three decisive criteria for inclusion were age, apostolicity and church-wide recognition, even though the compilation cannot be conclusively explained by them in every respect. The content of these writings was regarded as the existing "faith of the believers" since all differences were traced back to the central truths of salvation through the "one and guiding Spirit" (*pneuma hégemonikon*, Ps 51 {50}:14). Around 200 the canon of the New Testament had already been established for the congregations of the large churches insofar as the major writings and a general whole – the "New Testament" – had been recognized. There was, however, still uncertainty concerning the determination of the exact size. The "catholic" epistles first appeared in a "triple canon" (Jas, 1 Pet, 1 Jn); the enlargement to the "hepta-canon" seems to have migrated from the West to the East. Whether the apocalyptic literature belonged to the canon or not also remained unclear for quite some time; the Apocalypse of John first won general recognition in the West, then later in the East; and the "canonical" quality of the Epistle to the Hebrews remained uncertain for a long time.

This uncertainty still persisted in the fourth century. Eusebius made a distinction between recognized and disputed writings on the one hand (Jas, Jude, 2 Pet and 2 and 3 Jn) and pseudo-writings on the other (*Historia ecclesiae* III 25,3), whereas Athanasius cited our 27 books as "sources of salvation" of equal importance in which the "teaching of piety" is proclaimed (39th Easter Epistle from 367). But then, even this clear testimony cannot be taken as a definitive dictum for the whole Eastern church. The Syrian church, for example, adhered to a smaller canon of 22 New Testament books for a long time. In the Western church the canon of 27 books was established from the end of the fourth century on (the Synod of Rome, 382, the Synod of Hippo, 393). These "authoritative" decisions did not create new facts; they sanctioned instead the practice of the congregations and standardized them for the entire church.

4. The History of the Adoption of the Canon

4.1 Early Christianity did not at first adopt the Pharisaic theory of the canon that was in the process of being developed. The spread of the Christian faith in the Mediterranean area was largely based on the Greek translation of the Old Testament in the form of the extensive "Alexandrian" collection. But the growing dissimilarity to Judaism was also a contributing factor so that the Pharisaic attempt at the end of the first century to define the canon once and for all by reducing it to the 22 (24) books of the Hebrew Bible could not (yet) assert itself in the Christian world. Especially with respect to the third part of the Old Testament, the so-called "Writings", a relative openness of the canon boundary clearly existed. The New Testament authors quoted "holy Scripture" in the Greek version of the Septuagint in places where it deviated from the Hebrew text, and the New Testament and the Apostolic

Fathers used the deuterocanonical books in some places as "Scripture", i.e. applying the same formula for their citation. It seems that these texts even played a certain role in the development of the Son-of-Man Christology and the Wisdom-Christology.[4]

4.2 One can nevertheless observe how in the period following the "Hebrew canon" also had an effect on the attempts to delimit the Old Testament part of the Christian Bible more precisely. For example Melito of Sardes († 190) and the Synod of Laodicea (360) in the East as well as Hilary of Poitiers (315–368) and above all Jerome (347–420) in the West took the "Hebrew canon" as their starting point. By contrast, Augustine (354–430), who saw the canonicity of the deuterocanonical books justified by their use in most of the churches, can be seen as representative of the many *Greek and Latin Fathers* who held on to them. Athanasius (295–373) advocated an intermediate position which, to a large extent, gained acceptance in the East, but also – reinforced by Jerome – remained subliminally operative in the West. He made a clear distinction between the canonical books of the Hebrew collection and that group of additional writings of the Septuagint canon which, nevertheless, should also be read aloud in church instruction (*Anagignoskomena*).

4.3 The *Latin tradition*, taken as a whole, adopted the more extensive Septuagint collection and committed itself to it even more unequivocally than the East. The first formal "canonizations" of the Old Testament, including the deuterocanonical texts, took place at the Synods of Rome (382), Hippo (393) and Carthage (397 and 419). The *Decretum pro Jacobitis* at the Council of Florence reaffirmed once again the Septuagint (and Vulgate) version (DH 1334-1336 [cf. ND 208, "Decree for the Copts"]). Nevertheless, the theology before the Council of Trent did not answer questions with complete uniformity about the size of the canon in the Old Testament part or about the more exact demarcation of the canonical writings from the deuterocanonical texts. Influenced by humanism Erasmus of Rotterdam (1469–1536) as well

---

4   Cf. P. Stuhlmacher, "Die Bedeutung der Apokryphen und der Pseudepigraphen des Alten Testaments für das Verständnis Jesu und der Christologie," in: S. Meurer, ed., *Die Apokryphenfrage im ökumenischen Horizont*, Stuttgart 1989, pp. 13–25.

as Cardinal Cajetan (1469–1534) exhibited a tendency to limit the canon to the Hebrew canon. On the other hand there were still non-canonical texts like the *Prayer of Manasseh* and the third and fourth books of Esdras [1 Esd and 2 Esd in the NRSV] in the appendix of late medieval Vulgate editions as well as pre-Lutheran German editions of the Bible.[5]

4.4 *Martin Luther* likewise followed Jerome's judgment that one must distinguish clearly between the books of the Hebrew canon and those of the Greek canon. He tried, however, to set the boundary between the two groups less by means of formal criteria than on the basis of the content and its proximity to the gospel. His close correlation between a philological-historical and a theological appreciation of the texts allowed him on the one hand to take deuterocanonical ("apocryphal") books like Sirach, Wisdom and 1 Maccabees seriously as Holy Scripture and on the other hand to look critically at individual canonical books of the Hebrew canon, such as Esther. In addition Luther changed the order of the books of the Hebrew canon and brought it more in line with that of the Vulgate. Luther's canon-historical intervention was not reflected at first in the early Confessions.[6] With respect to the doctrine of Scripture, the Formula of Concord stated that "the prophetic and apostolic writings of the Old and New Testaments are the only rule and norm according to which all doctrines and teachers alike must be appraised and judged" (*The Book of Concord*, p. 464).

In early Protestant dogmatics, which had adopted the Hebrew canon theory, the first lists by name of the writings considered to be canonical and those considered to be "apocryphal" were provided – for example in the work of Martin Chemnitz (1522–1586). The opinion that the apocryphal texts should

---

5   Cf. K. D. Fricke, "Der Apokryphenteil der Lutherbibel," in: S. Meurer (note 4), pp. 51–82, here p. 61.
6   The "Apology of the Augsburg Confession" (no. 277–280 [in: *The Book of Concord: The Confessions of the Evangelical Lutheran Church*, transl. and ed. by T. G. Tappert, Philadelphia 1959, p. 148f.]) does not contest the scriptural authority of Tobit. The Zurich Bible of 1531 contains the books of the "entire bible according to the truth of the original Hebrew and Greek." The deuterocanonical texts are placed in the Old Testament after 2 Chronicles.

still be regarded as "useful and good to read" is evidenced, among other things, by the fact that the new edition of the Protestant lectionary of 1985 once again lists among the readings for the sermon sequences III–VI a whole series (24) of sermon pericopes from the deuterocanonical books.[7]

4.5 By contrast, an aversion to the deuterocanonical books developed in the Reformed church. *John Calvin's* critical position concerning the "apocrypha" was clearly discernible even before the decision of the Council of Trent on the canon question, but it was expressed even more emphatically afterwards in the form of dogmatic reservations ("Authority of the Council") and historical objections ("Contrary Testimonies of the Early Church"). In light of this background it is remarkable that Calvin drew specifically on deuterocanonical texts from time to time when he wanted to underscore theological convictions which were very important to him, such as the resurrection of the dead, immortality of the soul and the infiniteness of the Logos / of Wisdom. Seen as a whole, however, the absence of deuterocanonical texts in worship and their elimination from interpretations in sermons and lectures resulted in their gradual disappearance from the life of piety.[8]

4.6 *The Council of Trent*[9] tackled the fundamental problems of "Scripture and Tradition" right at the beginning of its detailed deliberations in February 1546 and dealt first of all with the clarification of the canon question. The Council Fathers confirmed the previous official Latin tradition in its entirety as last defined by the Council of Florence and approved a list of the individual books of the Vulgate ("with all their parts") on April 8, 1546. They thus reaffirmed the Septuagint canon without further explanations, but with a formal threat of anathema against divergent views (DH 1502–1504 [ND 211–213]). The council, therefore, made no attempt to justify the Florentine decision once again in a way that was in keeping with the times, nor did the

---

7 Cf. Fricke (note 5), p. 73.
8 Cf. W. H. Neuser, "Die Reformierten und die Apokryphen des Alten Testaments", in: Meurer, ed. (note 4), pp. 83–103, here especially pp. 98–100.
9 Concerning the following cf. H. Jedin, *Geschichte des Konzils von Trient*, vol. II, Freiburg 1957, pp. 42–82 [*A History of the Council of Trent*, vol. II, London 1961, pp. 52–98].

First Vatican Council, which explicitly accepted the decision of Trent (DH 3006, 3029 [ND 216, 218]), attempt to do this later. This course of action at Trent concealed an interesting council debate on the factual question. Several bishops who were familiar with the writings of the Reformation and humanism wished for a more detailed analysis of the objections raised in these texts, but they could not prevail. Nor did anything result from the discussion of whether one could do justice to the problems of the different historical traditions by assigning various "degrees of authority" within the canon. For example, the Augustinian superior general Seripando, who sympathized with the position of Erasmus and Cajetan, proposed a distinction between a (proto-canonical) *canon fidei* ("canonically authentic") and a (deuterocanonical) *canon morum* ("canonically ecclesiastical"), but his view was not accepted. The debates prove that there were widely divergent views within the council as well. For example that school of thought in pre-Tridentine theology was quite outspoken which regarded the deuterocanonical writings as belonging to the canon, but still wanted to limit their importance. In the end the majority opinion prevailed that "the council should not settle theological disputes which were already discussed between Augustine and Jerome, but should continue to leave them open."[10] The council thus committed itself "to the more extensive canon, but left ... the question about the differentiation of the books within the canon in its previous state."[11]

This different evaluation of the books within the established limits of the Septuagint canon also seems to have persisted in the practice of the Catholic church.[12] For example, in the wake of the liturgy reform of the Second Vatican Council the new order of readings includes only 10 texts from deuterocanonical books for the Sundays and the Holy Days in the entire three-year cycle (Wisdom and Sirach appear together seven times, Baruch twice, and 2 Maccabees once).

---

10 Jedin, *Geschichte* (note 9), p. 46.
11 Ibid.
12 Cf. F. J. Stendebach, "Der Kanon des Alten Testaments in der katholischen Kirche," in: Meurer, ed. (note 4), pp. 41–50, here p. 49.

The complex tradition is reflected in the views of the *Orthodox Churches*[13] insofar as various positions can still be found. The Greek Orthodox Church, for example, denies the canonicity of the deuterocanonical texts; in contrast they appear in the biblical canons of the Coptic, the Ethiopian, the Syrian and the Armenian Orthodox Church. Deuterocanonical texts play an important role in the religious consciousness of the East because they were used and mentioned by the early church theologians and are used in hymns and iconography as well. But taken as a whole, the position of Athanasius, a sort of "middle ground," has determined the direction over time. The seventeenth century discussion – resumed not least of all as a result of the encounter with Protestantism – concerning the question of how one should treat the contradictory definitions of the Synods of Laodicea and Carthage was also inconclusive. For example, the Synod of Constantinople (1642) designated the deuterocanonical texts as "not canonical," but declared at the same time that they were of good and virtuous content and should not be abandoned.

The theoretical distinction between the "canonical" books and "instructional books" is therefore upheld in the Orthodox churches, but apparently without any great practical significance.

5. Conclusions

5.1 Looking back at the *history* we can state that both forms of the canon originally sprang from Jewish (Hebraic-Aramaic) roots.

The more extensive scriptural collection of the Septuagint and the Vulgate corresponds to a great extent to the "Holy Scripture" of the first Christians and thus maintains a closeness to the language and the conceptual world of the New Testament which were greatly influenced by the Hellenistic Judaism of antiquity.

---

13 On this point cf. E. Oikonomos, "Die Bedeutung der deuterokanonischen Schriften in der orthodoxen Kirche," in: Meurer, ed. (note 4), pp. 137–145, esp. pp. 140–143.

By contrast, the more limited canon of the Hebrew Bible manifests a clearer connection to contemporary Judaism which has, right up to the present, adhered to the Pharisaic determination of the canon in the first century C.E.

Each of the two traditions has its own Christian history of transmission, and each of these has had multiple contacts with the other. If one takes these historical links and exertions of influences seriously with respect to the origin as well as the transmission of the two different determinations of the canon, then the theological importance of the difference between them can no longer be ascertained simply by comparing them in a formal, numerical way.

5.2 Rather, the decisive question is the one concerning the *theological* significance of the emergence of an "Old" Testament, that is, the question about the importance of the insight that the history of the words and actions of the living God reflected in these texts first reaches its completion with respect to salvation history in the spirit-wrought "Christ event."

Early Christendom answered this question with the firm belief that the multiform and tension-filled experience of God attested and preserved in the texts of the "Old Testament" is already an expression of that divine love and care which became efficacious in a new and unparalleled fashion in the life and fate of Jesus of Nazareth. It was convinced that as a result the entire history of God with human beings appears in a concentrated way in Jesus and is therefore "viewed all at once" in the post-Easter declaration of belief in Christ (Heb 1:1–4; Col 1:12–20; Eph 1:3–14; Phil 2:5–11). In such a total Christian view it is not only not out of the question, but in fact presupposed that the "canon of the Old Testament writings" is not a self-contained entity, but is instead open to the further salvation history and its attestation in the New Testament texts, just as the testimony to the saving action of God in Jesus Christ is dependent on the witness of the Old Testament.

This faith-based awareness that the two divine "testaments" intrinsically refer to each other can make it possible for us contemporary Christians of different denominations to recognize the theological importance of the "deuterocanonical" books, which were accepted in the early church, in their historical function as a bridge between the jointly approved books of the "canon of the Hebrew Bible" and the undisputed "canon of the books of the New Testament."

5.3 As a *practical consequence* the "Guidelines for Interconfessional Cooperation in Translating the Bible," which were adopted in 1987 by the Roman Secretariat for Promoting Christian Unity and the United Bible Societies, propose that complete Bibles in the future contain all the books of the Septuagint canon with the deuterocanonical books (and parts of books) appearing as a separate block before the New Testament. Such an arrangement would indeed take both traditions into account in an appropriate manner. Moreover, these guidelines prefer to use the designation "deuterocanonical" rather than the word "apocryphal" which is used in a different sense and is thus ambiguous. In all the denominations "deuterocanonical" is probably the term which can best ensure the desired clarity in the designation of those books which have been handed down in the Septuagint version in addition to the books of the "Hebrew Bible."

5.4 Besides considering the history of the canon, we should pay greater attention to the use of Scripture in worship according to the order of readings of the church calendar. Which preconditions and intentions guide the assignment of the readings from the Old Testament, the epistles and the gospels? Where is there accord, where are there differences and what weight do these carry? An agreement among the churches on the cycles of readings would be possible and desirable.[14]

III. Fundamental Considerations

1. Ecumenical Convergences

1.1 Remarkable agreements or advances in understanding are emerging in the ecumenical dialogue on the topics "Canon – Scripture – Tradition." There

---

14 Cf. G. Lathrop and G. Ramshaw, eds., *Lectionary for the Christian People: Cycle A–C of the Roman, Episcopal, Lutheran Lectionaries*, Philadelphia 1986–1988.

is agreement that Holy Scripture is sufficient for salvation and does not need to be supplemented in terms of content by additional church traditions. It is true that the Tridentine doctrine that the saving truth and moral teaching of the gospel is contained in written books and unwritten traditions (*in libris scriptis et sine scripto traditionibus*), both of which deserve to be accepted and venerated with the same sense of devotion and reverence (*pari pietatis affectu ac reverentia*), has often been interpreted as a theory of two testimonies of revelation which complement each other in a material way.[15] But this interpretation of Trent's teaching is by no means conclusive – especially in the light of the hermeneutics of the Constitution on Divine Revelation of the Second Vatican Council. Even if one keeps to its express language the text from the Council of Trent does "not, as has so often occurred, have to be understood in the sense that the truth of the gospel is partly contained in Sacred Scripture and partly in tradition. One can also understand the council statement in the sense of the Church Fathers and the great theologians of the High Middle Ages: Sacred Scripture contains all of faith in its substance, but this faith can only be grasped in its entirety and fullness in light of tradition."[16] In any case, after largely effective historical research it is certain that the thesis of the material sufficiency of the Bible was not condemned in Trent. The statement in *Dei Verbum* 9 remains controversial if it is interpreted as a rejection of the Reformation formula *sola scriptura*; it must also be discussed even further in the context of tradition and the teaching office. But there are good reasons for understanding this statement as follows: Certitude about the revelation testified to in Scripture is conveyed through its proclamation, preservation and dissemination in the church. According to *Dei Verbum* 10 the teaching office of the church remains subordinate to the authority of Scripture as the word of God.

In the meantime the thesis concerning the material sufficiency of Scripture has gained wide acceptance in contemporary Catholic theology and proven to be objectively convincing. As a result Catholic and Protestant theologians

---

15 Talk about two "sources of revelation" does not correspond to the statement of the Council of Trent: cf. DH 1501 [ND 210].
16 *Das Glaubensbekenntnis der Kirche*, Kevelaer, Munich, Stuttgart, Limburg, Regensburg, Cologne 1985, p. 54, in reference to *Dei Verbum* 9.

can jointly testify that Sacred Scripture contains the whole truth of faith necessary for salvation and makes it possible for this truth to be understood as such. Since it is sufficient in a material sense, it can function as a criterion for the gospel-conformity of all church proclamation and the entire life of the church. Consequently the relationship between Scripture and tradition should not be represented as that of two complementary sources of revelation. Instead there is only one source of salvation, namely God's revelation manifest in the Spirit in Jesus Christ, the crucified and risen one, as it is witnessed in the apostolic proclamation as gospel and documented in Holy Scripture in a materially sufficient way.

1.2 Considerable progress toward agreement is also emerging with respect to the concept of tradition itself and the problem of correctly determining the relationship between Scripture and tradition. At the Council of Trent it was still not completely clear whether tradition or traditions should be thought of as pertaining only to apostolic writings or also to other customs which had come into practice in the course of church history. An alternative determination of Scripture and tradition had become common in the Protestant world because the concept of tradition, for instance in the *Augsburg Confession*, did not primarily refer to the church's body of tradition contained in the gospel of Jesus Christ or to its prevailing mediation in the historical course of time, but instead and above all to mere human rules and regulations as distinct from the divine promise or the divine commandment. The results from terminological investigations prove this unequivocally. Whereas the singular form *traditio* is used only once in the Latin text of the *Augsburg Confession*, following the usage of the Vulgate (*Augsburg Confession* XXVI.22), this Latin version mentions *traditiones* 27 times (*Augsburg Confession* XV.4; XXVI.3, 6, 8 {twice}, 12 {twice}, 13, 14, 15, 16, 19, 40; XXVIII.35, 37, 39, 42 {twice}, 43, 46, 47, 49 {twice}, 64, 67, 68, 69), and mostly in the sense denoted by the phrases *traditiones humanae* or *traditiones hominum* (cf. *Augsburg Confession* VII.3; XV.3, XXVI.1, 5, 21; XXVIII.74). Accordingly, *traditiones* are practices which are merely prescribed by ecclesiastical authority and not commanded by the word of Holy Scripture. "The *Augsburg Confession* counts among these the fasting laws of the church, liturgical regulations, religious life, brotherhoods, pilgrimages, the veneration of the saints, praying the rosary, days of abstinence, liturgical regulations for vestments, Sunday observance, as well as the holy days of obligation."[17] This fact is verified by the German text of the *Augsburg Confession*: The term "tradition", which is used in seven places (*Bekenntnisschriften der evangelisch-lutherischen Kirche*, lateinischer und deutscher Text, Göttingen 1992, 70.3; 83d.20; 100.15; 101.16; 104.1 and 8; 106.25), being explicitly defined more precisely as "human tradition" in two instances (ibid., 101.16; 104.8) as well as occasionally exchanged for the plural form in the different editions of the text (and vice versa), always denotes "human regulations." Although their relative value is not disputed, their elevation to being "obligatory or even something necessary for salvation" is rigorously opposed.[18]

The Reformation's treatment of the theme of tradition, however, is not exhausted with the judgment that traditions are human regulations. Besides using the verb form *tradere* three times (cf. XX.22, XXVII.48, 57), which is attributed to the proclamation and preaching of the gospel as well as to the divine mandate grounded in the events of revelation, the *Augsburg Confession* resolutely adopts the so-called early church tradition – the witness of the Church Fathers and especially the symbols of the early church. It is true that, according to the confession of the Reformation, this early church tradition does not represent an authority coordinated to the gospel witnessed in Scripture, but is instead a function of scriptural witness for teaching the correct perception of it. It does not usurp the role of being the prescribing norm which belongs to Scripture alone. This does not, however, argue against the fact that according to Protestant conviction as well Scripture and tradition (in the sense of passing down the apostolic proclamation) belong inseparably together.

---

17 B. Dittrich, *Das Traditionsverständnis in der Confessio Augustana und in der Confutatio*, Leipzig 1983, p. 16f. in reference to the *Augsburg Confession* XX: 3; XXVI: 2, 8; XXVIII: 30.
18 A. Sperl, "Zur Geschichte des Begriffes 'Tradition' in der Evangelischen Theologie", in: W. Andersen (ed.), *Das Wort Gottes in Geschichte und Gegenwart*, Munich 1957, pp, 147–159, quote p. 151.

Given the history of the concept "tradition" and the word's semantic changes, it does not contradict the Protestant understanding of the significance of Holy Scripture to say: Scripture, which became canonical after evolving in a long transmission process in the sphere of the church, is itself a form of tradition, namely the form of apostolic proclamation, including its foundations in the writings of the Old Testament, which remains authoritative. Similarly it does not contradict the Roman Catholic understanding of Scripture to say: Scripture is the criterion for the validity of all church traditions.

We must of course hold on to the distinction between God's word and human words even for Scripture's permanently authoritative form of tradition and still more for church traditions. We should also adhere to the criterion by which teaching and practice in the church are deemed either in keeping with or contrary to the gospel. An agreement on these matters will have to include a determination of the relationship between spirit and letter as well as law and gospel. The existing, shared approaches for determining these relationships (Augustine, Thomas Aquinas, Luther et al.) should then be treated in view of the judging and saving effect of God's word.

2. The Canonicity of the Canon and Its Justification

If Scripture and tradition belong together as described, the pertinent disputes of the past can be consolidated into two closely connected factual aspects: the problem of justifying the canonicity of the canon, and the problem of interpreting Scripture authentically. Indisputably the Christian canon was formed in the context of proclamation, believing and professing, thus in particular within the framework of the worship of the congregation, so that it is possible to say that the lived life of the church was instrumental in forming the canon. For this reason there can be no question of a fundamental opposition between Scripture and the church. It is also undeniable that the evolution of the canon of Scripture was a prolonged, complex and differentiated developmental process. Moreover, the finally canonized scriptures represent among themselves and within themselves quite different forms of tradition which also carry different weights from a factual point of view. The problem of the canon's objective continuity and identity resulting from the historical fact of the canonical process cannot be solved by assuming the existence of a formal, authoritative instance which, so to speak from a position external to Scripture and on its own, would guarantee the unity of the canon and the certainty of its canonicity. Nor can we solve the problem by taking the canon out of historical contexts in an ahistorical-fundamentalist way. On the contrary, justified certainty with respect to the canonicity of the canon can only be achieved if criteria can be found in the actual course of the history of the canon as well as in the tradition-historical genesis and the explicit content of the individual canonical texts. These criteria enable us to reconstruct and to explore both the history of the canon as a whole and the meaning of individual canonical texts on the basis of factual judgments of quality. For New Testament texts such criteria are closeness to the source (apostolicity) and factual adequacy (conformity to Christ); for the biblical texts as a whole the criteria are the agreement of their testimony in an inner core of meaning (identity of the Old Testament God with the father of Jesus Christ) as well as their dissemination in the congregations and the consensus existing in these concerning their normativeness. These criteria can be applied without difficulty to the vast majority of the canonical books of the Old and the New Testament. Their application, however, does not rule out that individual books elude a justification which would make their inclusion in or exclusion from the canon certain – a fact that is reflected in their differently weighted use in worship as well as in the controversial theological positions concerning the canon question. Still there is agreement that the determination of the canon did not simply occur in a formal, juridical manner, but according to inner criteria and material factors based on an understanding and an interpretation which derived from the content of the ultimately canonized writings.

With this in mind the Catholic side can also say both that the canon in its central core commands our respect and that considerable historical and objective truth supports the theory of the self-assertion of the canon, even though such self-assertion did not occur with all the texts to the same extent. This is the basic prerequisite for maintaining that there can also be a critical authority of Scripture today and in the future vis-à-vis the church and its formulated doctrinal statements as explicitly recognized by the Catholic Church and Catholic theology.

In turn, the Protestant side does not deny, but explicitly confirms that the church had to make decisions in particular about the exclusion of texts and the delimitation of the canon, just as church doctrinal statements and pastoral officials in congregations in general played an important part in the entire process of canonization. The theory of the self-assertion of the canon seeks to convey the insight that the actual contribution of church office-holders, which is historically indisputable, can only be judged appropriate and permanently binding if that contribution was consistent with criteria based on an understanding of the matter which were communicable and comprehensible by means of reasoned argument and derived from the content of the ultimately canonized texts. This is the basic prerequisite for maintaining that the Protestant Church and Protestant theology must not view the contribution of even formal-juridical and authoritative acts of the official church to the process of the history of the canon as a contradiction of their fundamental conviction that the biblical canon is self-assertive.

It is to be added that the gospel's becoming Scripture is an inner moment of the completed event of revelation. Consequently, in this respect as well Sacred Scripture participates in the normative character of revelation which is fundamental for all tradition. Likewise it must hold true in general and theologically on principle that the church did not produce Scripture in a causative sense, but received it as God's word through the power of the Holy Spirit. Therefore, in the act of forming the canon the post-apostolic church placed itself resolutely under Scripture as canon; indeed, the very act of forming the canon was already the result of unquestionable certitude about the objective meaning of the ultimately canonized texts.

3. The Size of the Canon

As with the canonicity of the canon as a whole, we can only make a decision about its concrete size or about the number of texts collected in it on the basis of content-related criteria. At the same time we must rule out the assumption right from the start that an indefinite openness exists since only a limited canon in terms of quantity can attest historical revelation. There is in fact widespread agreement among the denominations concerning the canon question. A difference actually exists only as to the size of the Old Testament canon which is linked to the question, which arose in the 16th century, about how this should be decided. Whereas the Council of Trent, confirming prior magisterial decisions, defined the canon in precise terms, there was originally on the Protestant side no official ecclesiastical determination and numerical listing of the individual canonical books – apart from the actual corpus in the Protestant editions of the Bible and the order and prioritization of the biblical books presented there. The *French Confession of Faith* (1559), art. 3f., the *Belgic Confession* (1561), art. 4ff., each of which laid down a canon catalog, and the *Confessio Helvetica posterior* (1566), art. 1 are exceptions; they jointly state that faith is not to be based on the Apocrypha. The other confessional writings of the Reformation deliberately do not speak of a numerical self-quantification, but of the *testimonium Spiritus Sancti internum* which provides criteria for a delimitation of the canon in terms of content. – Therefore the Reformation's assumption that there is a qualitative self-assertion of the canon does not in every case imply its definitive self-quantification. While the Protestant fathers certainly wanted to preserve the codified form of the Bible as a definite, quantifiable whole, a definitive fixation of the corpus of sacrosanct texts, including accepting that all the texts regarded as canonical had equal authoritative status, occurred on the whole only in reaction to the Council of Trent and in the course of the formalization of the scriptural principle effected, at least in a broad sense, by the dogmatics of early Protestant orthodoxy.

The material reasons underlying these historical findings should be taken into account if an agreement is to be reached regarding the prescribed or customary canon-catalogs of the churches. The following aspects can be helpful here. The idea suggested by the Reformation that the completed state of the canon must not be understood in a legal sense should enable Protestant theologians to consider the scriptures denominated the Old Testament Apocrypha (which, according to Protestant usage, should be distinguished from the *pseudepigrapha*) as having a place among the canonical texts, especially since there are valid tradition-historical reasons for this and since important Reformation editions of the Bible printed the apocryphal texts. Even more important, the corpus of the *graphé* quoted in the New Testament scriptures is to a large extent the Old Testament in its Septuagint form. Conversely Roman Catholic theologians should not only be permitted, but in fact ought to regard the context of canonical texts as differentiated in many ways, not least of which in a qualitative respect. Such a perception is not opposed to the legitimate demand to take all of Scripture in all its parts seriously; instead, as a necessary implication of every concrete use of Scripture, it fulfills this demand.

4. The Problem of Authentic Scriptural Interpretation

It is indisputable that we can only decide about the authenticity of scriptural interpretation on the basis of what Scripture itself says. Consequently only the text of Scripture itself can be the criterion for its correct perception. To the extent that the Reformation's assumption of a "self-interpretation" of Scripture aims at the objectivity of the scriptural content that precedes all subjective forms of interpretation as well as at the obvious unity of the total meaning of Scripture, it is shared by Roman Catholic theology. There is also agreement that an interpretation of Scripture which claims authenticity must primarily be oriented towards and proven by the literal sense of Scripture. Here the individual passage must be seen within the total context of the canon. Furthermore both Protestants and Catholics assume that accepting an objective standard of scriptural interpretation grounded in Scripture itself implies accepting externally and internally that at least the core content of scripture is clear and capable of self-authentication. Here the *claritas externa* is guaranteed by the aforementioned literal sense of Scripture, and the *claritas interna* by the self-transmission and self-authentication (*autopistie*) of Jesus Christ which are both operative in the *sensus literalis* through the power of the Holy Spirit.

It is acceptable and meaningful to talk about a "self-interpretation" of Scripture, however, only if the self-interpretation does not exclude, but includes the activity of the interpreter or interpreters in the process of understanding.

The truth of Scripture only proves itself in the act of being perceived so that one cannot properly speak of a self-interpretation of Scripture without that perception which is concretely located in the church. Protestant theology shares this view and acknowledges that a suitable use of Scripture is only possible in the community of the church where communication occurs and responsibility is shared in the unity of the Spirit of Christ. The word and the truth of God would not really have arrived in the world had they not been accepted in the faith of the people and witnessed to publicly through the power of this very same Holy Spirit. In this respect the content of the word of God cannot be separated from the worldly forms of both the interpretation and the proclamation of the word according to Sacred Scripture.

On the basis of these agreements the traditional controversial theological differences should certainly be limited, if they cannot be removed altogether, and reduced to the problems which have not yet been adequately clarified concerning authorities responsible for providing certitude in a binding way, and in particular to the role of the teaching office in the process of the interpretation of Scripture.

5. Frame of Reference for Contemporary Ecumenical Teaching on Scripture

5.1 With its insistence on "verbal inspiration" the scriptural teaching of post-Reformation dogmatics emphasized the principle of the indissoluble unity of spirit and letter in the external words of Scripture. This unity is grounded in Holy Scripture and has at all times been confirmed by the Christian church. The principle was stressed in particular in opposition to views which maintained that the words of Scripture had no power in themselves so that the influence of the Spirit still had to be added to the letter and the text to inspire people. In its intent this differentiation within the Reformation, especially as it was formulated in the Rahtmann Dispute, is similar to the differentiation from and rejections of Enthusiasm in article V of the *Augsburg Confession* and in part III, article VIII of the *Schmalkald Articles* [cf. *The Book of Concord*, p. 31 and p. 312f.]. Typical of Enthusiasm was the view that the Spirit stood apart from or over above the external words in order to make them effective and intelligible.

5.2 Roman Catholic theology reacted to the Reformation's teaching on Scripture by emphasizing that scriptural statements vary and are in need of interpretation and by stressing the active role of the church and the church's magisterium both in the formation of the canon and in the interpretation of Scripture. Within this framework Catholic theology developed important approaches to the historical criticism of the Bible in the 17th century.

5.3 Under the weight of the steadily growing number of insights with respect to the contingent nature of biblical statements as a result of their human-historical character, the Protestant theology of the 17th and 18th centuries could no longer adhere to the objective unity of Scripture's letter, spirit, and teaching which had been claimed in the classical Protestant doctrine of Scripture. The evolving literary criticism of Scripture and the observation of contradictory statements in biblical texts contributed to this, as did tensions between biblical statements and the developing scientific world view. The theory of the Holy Spirit's accommodation to the historically contingent and restricted conditions of understanding of the biblical authors had been developed in defense of the doctrine of inspiration, but it actually led to the erosion of this doctrine. Especially the assumption that the biblical writings exhibit doctrinal unity could not be maintained on the basis of their historical interpretation. This created a new situation for the theologies of both Protestant and Catholic traditions and for their relationship to each other.

5.4 To the degree that the newer Protestant theology opened itself up to historical-critical exegesis it was no longer able to establish the doctrinal unity of the biblical testimonies directly from the words of Scripture. Instead it had to resort to the subjectivity of an interpreter. Either the subjective piety of the individual interpreter or the collective subjectivity, as it were, of the confessional traditions which were valid and authoritative in the churches became the hermeneutical principle here. The criticism of the doctrine of verbal inspiration, however, threatened to dissolve the connection between spirit and letter in the external words of the Bible. But even where a unified biblical theology was proposed contrary to historical-critical exegesis, Scripture was in fact interpreted and conceived as a doctrinal unity from the viewpoint of the subjectivity of the theological interpreter. Either way the role of the interpreter's subjectivity with respect to the question of the doctrinal content of Scripture could no longer be avoided.

5.5 Thus from their different starting points the denominational positions were actually converging in the question of the interpretation of Scripture without invalidating the Protestant opposition to the Catholic claim that the church's teaching office has final, decisive authority to interpret. Catholics connected the role of subjectivity in the interpretive process to the principle of tradition. The hierarchical magisterium, academic theology, and the sense of faith of the faithful were considered to be instruments of the tradition process. The magisterium was understood as an exceptionally qualified authenticating authority. As subjective bearer of the tradition process it could virtually be identified with tradition in the extreme case. The logic of this development lies in the consistent perception of the problem of providing a binding justification for certainty about the content of Scripture in the particular place where it is used and interpreted. The danger here, which cannot be overlooked, is the possibility that Scripture might be disqualified from being an authority critical of church office should the need arise.

5.6 The adoption of the historical-critical method in Catholic biblical exegesis at the beginning of the 20th century first met with fierce reactions from the teaching office of the church. Nonetheless the reception of the historical-critical method was so sweeping in the following decades – especially since Pius XII's encyclical *Divino afflante spiritu* in 1943 – that today there are almost no denominationally conditioned differences whatsoever in the field of biblical exegesis. The theologies of both churches are confronted with solving the following hermeneutical problem arising from this development: Under the conditions of historical-critical exegesis how can the unity of Scripture as a canon of the Old and the New Testament be discerned in a new way, and the revelatory action of God's Spirit which is at work in it be explicitly understood and emphasized? A huge ecumenical opportunity lies in the shared character of this task.

5.7 On the one hand the Second Vatican Council integrated the historical interpretation of the Bible into a comprehensive understanding of God's revelation. On the other hand it tried to confront the danger of Scripture being deprived of its independence by placing the teaching office in all its forms under the existing authority of the word of God and assigning to it the task of serving the word of God. In so doing it also put the magisterium into the context of the life of the people of God. Church teaching conforms to its concept and essence only if it is appropriate to scriptural witness. At the same time the authority to interpret Scripture authentically which, according to Roman Catholic belief, has been given to the teaching office of the church, does not pertain first and foremost to individual biblical passages, but to the overall context of the word of God. The church emphasizes here that this overall context should be perceived only in a communicative and dialogical way, taking into account the sense of faith of the entire people of God which is bound to the word of Scripture. This development from the Second Vatican Council touches original and central concerns of the Reformation. According to the Protestant view authentic interpretation of Scripture also takes place in the sphere of the church, namely through preaching and teaching the gospel with reference to the confession of the church. Here the authenticity of the interpretation of Scripture is grounded on the material or factual authority of the biblical content itself as it is revealed in the letter of Scripture through the power of the Spirit proceeding from God's self-revelation in Jesus Christ and makes itself felt in the consciences of the hearers of the word. Thus according to the teaching of the Reformation the spiritual authority of Scripture in the process of its interpretation also refers to the overall context of the scriptural witness, to the "central matter" of Scripture, and makes itself felt in a communicative event. But at the same time the teaching of the Reformation stresses that the interpretation is bound to the literal sense of scriptural statements. In the end, therefore, that literal sense is the standard by which the authenticity and authority of ecclesial interpretations as well as every magisterial interpretation of Scripture are measured. At the same time it is the right and duty of every believer to form an opinion based on facts about the doctrinal proclamation of the church by reading and studying Scripture itself. Consequently, the principles of the Reformation's teaching on Scripture not only make it impossible for the ecclesiastical office to proclaim a doctrine which is not authenticated by scriptural witness, but also refute the assumption that an individual member or group of members of the church can, on the basis of their office or person, authoritatively claim to decide alone about the legitimate interpretation of Scripture. This does not rule out that, according to the Reformation's view, there is also a special responsibility attached to the ecclesiastical office to "judge doctrine and condemn doctrine that is contrary to the Gospel" (*Augsburg Confession* XXVIII.21 [The Book of Concord, p. 84]). Since every doctrinal proclamation of the church remains subject to the judgment of the faithful as to whether it agrees with Scripture, there is an irreducible plurality of active subjects in the process of scriptural interpretation. As understood by the Reformation, the unity of the central matter of Scripture asserts itself precisely in the plurality of the interpretations, although only in the form of a process of interpretation, criticism and reception.

5.8 The question of whether insurmountable denominational differences exist today between the Reformation and the Roman Catholic view concerning the issues of the authority and interpretation of Scripture depends in a decisive way on the following conditions: on the one hand on whether one accepts or rejects that there is a critical function of Scripture, which is to be literally interpreted, in relation to doctrinal statements of the church teaching office; and on the other hand on whether one affirms or negates that the preaching ministry of the church has a function in the interpretation of Scripture. If the authority of Scripture as God's word cannot be correctly described apart from its use in the proclamation or preaching of the church because the unity of word and spirit can only be preserved in this way, then the theology of the Reformation will not be able to relegate the interpretation of Scripture solely to the scholarly exegesis of the Bible. Instead it will recognize the doctrinal proclamation of the church as the place and the occasion where the central matter of Scripture is proclaimed in its identity, which is both decisive and binding for faith, as the word of God. This proclamation may occur at different levels of discourse representing the church, but it always remains subject to the judgment of the faithful as a whole and to the judgment of each individual thereof, as well as subject to the scrutiny of theology with respect to its correspondence to the literal meaning of scriptural statements. Moving beyond the declarations of the Second Vatican Council, Catholics should acknowledge to a greater degree this role of the reception of church teaching by the people of God and the simultaneous scrutiny of it by means of the testimony of Scripture. In the process one does not need to exclude either a critical function of the letter of Scripture over against church teaching, whose form is always historically conditioned, or the necessity of interpreting the statements of the teaching office ever anew on the basis of the witness of Scripture. Both result from the claim that the teaching office serves the word of God – it does not stand above it, but allows itself to be led by it. If the implications of this claim are considered more precisely, also with respect to the critical function of scriptural interpretation in the church and for the further development of the church's doctrinal proclamation, then it should be possible to reach an agreement on the questions which are still open between the churches with regard to this matter.

Ecumenical Study Group of Protestant and Catholic Theologians

The Understanding and Use of Scripture

Concluding Report

1 Introduction: The Ecumenical Context and Our Objective

1.1 Our Shared Conviction

(1) The doctrine of Holy Scripture has been disputed between the denominations since the time of the Reformation. How one should understand the authority of Scripture was controversial, but at issue in particular were its interpretation and the role of the offices responsible for its binding interpretation. The differences relating to these matters have determined the theological tradition and formation of doctrine in both churches. These differences also surfaced repeatedly as we worked on various topics in our Ecumenical Study Group. In the meantime, however, our impression has been reinforced that the former differences in the understanding of Scripture are diminishing today as a result of our growing agreement in the praxis of scriptural exegesis as well as in the theological doctrine of Scripture.

(2) The document "Scripture, Tradition and Traditions" of the Fourth World Conference of the "Commission for Faith and Order" in Montreal in 1963 can also serve as an expression of our shared conviction: "Thus we can say that we exist as Christians by the Tradition of the Gospel (the *paradosis* of the *kerygma*) testified in Scripture, transmitted in and by the Church through the power of the Holy Spirit. Tradition taken in this sense is actualized in the preaching of the Word, in the administration of sacraments and worship, in

Christian teaching and theology, and in mission and witness to Christ by the lives of the members of the Church."[19]

(3) Connected in this way to all Christian churches, we have tried to achieve a better understanding of the denominationally determined Protestant and Catholic approaches to Holy Scripture. In the thematic areas of "the understanding of Scripture" and "the use of Scripture" we have determined what we have in common and which differences remain, and we are now presenting our findings to the public.

At the outset we would like to call to mind the efforts of other ecumenical committees which preceded our own. Our project "Binding Testimony," which concludes with this text, is connected to preceding studies by our own group, and it is in the context of these that the specific orientation of the present dialogue document can be discerned.

1.2 The Previous Ecumenical Discussions

(4) *Since the beginning of the Ecumenical Movement* an important precondition for the agreement being sought was the conviction that Christians possess a common foundation in the biblical texts for their struggle for the true form of Christian faith and life which is binding for the church.

This was evident at the Third Plenary Session of the World Council of Churches in New Delhi in 1961 where the assembled delegates[20] expressly approved an expansion of the basic formula of the WCC as "a fellowship of churches which confess the Lord Jesus Christ as God and Savior *according*

---

19 "Scripture, Tradition and Traditions," 1963, no. 45, quoted in: E. Flesseman-van Leer, ed., *The Bible: Its Authority and Interpretation in the Ecumenical Movement*, Geneva 1980, p. 20.

20 For the first time Orthodox churches from the socialist countries as well as many African and Asian churches were also represented there, and the Secretariat for Promoting Christian Unity, established in 1960, sent five official Roman Catholic observers.

to the Scriptures, and therefore seek to fulfill together their common calling to the glory of the one God, Father, Son and Holy Spirit."[21] In the multilateral ecumenical dialogue on the global level the "Faith and Order Commission" in particular has addressed the thematic areas which can be combined under the heading "The Bible and the Church's Interpretation of Scripture."[22]

Ecumenical consideration of the denominationally determined approaches to the biblical scriptures and examination of the views with respect to the authority of these texts in the life of the church already spans decades. The general development of the theological exegesis of Scripture in the second half of the 20th century has certainly exerted an influence here. That can be seen, for instance, in the fact that the profession of the unity of witness of both testaments, which had been poignantly formulated in an early text[23], was not at first repeated in the 1950's and 60's as a result of the deepened recognition of the multiformity and variable nature of biblical texts[24]. In the

---

21 Cf. F. Lüpsen, ed., *Neu Delhi Dokumente. Berichte und Reden auf der Weltkonferenz in Neu Delhi 1961*, 2nd edition, Witten 1962, p. 475.

22 Cf. M. Haudel. *Die Bibel und die Einheit der Kirchen. Eine Untersuchung der Studien von "Glauben und Kirchenverfassung,"* Göttingen 1993 (bibliography). The most important documents can be found in: E. Flesseman-van Leer, ed., *The Bible* (note 1). Among these are the following: "Scripture, Tradition and Traditions" (Montreal 1963); "The Significance of the Hermeneutical Problem for the Ecumenical Movement" (Bristol 1967); "The Authority of the Bible" (Louvain 1971); "How Does the Church Teach Authoritatively Today?" (Odessa 1977); "The Significance of the Old Testament in its Relation to the New" (Bangalore 1978).

23 Cf. "Guiding Principles for the Interpretation of the Bible," Faith and Order, 1949, quoted in: E. Flesseman-van Leer, ed., *The Bible* (note 19), p. 14: "It is agreed that the unity of the Old and the New Testaments is not to be found in any naturalistic development, or in any static identity, but in the ongoing redemptive activity of God in the history of one people, reaching its fulfilment in Christ."

24 Cf. "The Significance of the Hermeneutical Problem for the Ecumenical Movement," Faith and Order, 1967, quoted in: E. Flesseman-van Leer, ed., *The Bible* (note 19), p. 31f.: "The Bible contains a collection of very diverse literary traditions, the contents of which often stand in tension with one another. The diversity constitutes one of the main problems for the theological understanding of the Bible.... The diversity of thought within the Bible reflects the diversity of God's actions in different histori-

recent past, however, this formulation has reappeared in the dialogue papers under new circumstances.[25]

Of particular importance was the shared belief reached in the 1960's that the biblical writings themselves should be understood as an element of church tradition – as "Tradition in its written form"[26]; these Scriptures are permanently dependent on a living process of transmission in which one must ensure that the one Tradition is preserved in the different church traditions. With the intensified efforts since the 1980's to reach a consensus concerning the central questions of church life, the topic of the "Binding Interpretation of Scripture" remained on the ecumenical agenda.

(5) *In the international bilateral discussions* conducted by the denominations with increasing frequency since the 1970's the appeal to Holy Scripture as the norm of Christian faith has been a starting point. It has been very important to strengthen this foundation, particularly in the inaugural phase of the dialogues. The prospect that participants will be able to explain their essential agreement concerning belief in Jesus Christ by reflecting on the biblical testimony[27] as well as the insight that further steps towards each other do not

---

cal situations and the diversity of human response to God's actions. It is important that the scholar should not attach himself to one facet of biblical thought, however central it seems to him to be, in such a way as to cut himself off from this variety and richness. Although the truth in Christ is one, the human witness to it is manifold."

25 Cf. "The Significance of the Old Testament in its Relation to the New," Faith and Order, 1978, no. 19, quoted in: E. Flesseman-van Leer, ed., *The Bible* (note 19), p. 66: "The Bible is a collection of many varied books which in their two collections are held together by one subject. We meet in them one and the same God in his dealings with his whole creation, with the nations and with individual people. It is he who creates the unity in the diverse testimonies of Old and New Testaments." Ellen Flesseman-van Leer talks about a renewed "interest in the theological unity of the Bible" in the 1970's (ibid., "Introduction", p. 10).
26 "Scripture, Tradition and Traditions," Faith and Order, 1963, no. 50, quoted in: E. Flesseman-van Leer, ed., *The Bible* (note 19), p. 21.
27 This is how the Joint Commission of the Roman Catholic Church and the World Council of the Methodist Churches determined their "essential agreement on the Bible as God's living Word" in 1971 and formulated the task of "clarifying some of the

appear to be possible without an agreement on the authority of Scripture[28] both suggest that rounds of dialogue should begin with a discussion of each side's understanding of revelation and Scripture.

In many bilateral dialogues in which the Roman Catholic Church participated certain statements of the Second Vatican Council were also considered helpful for reaching an agreement in the thematic areas of "Scripture and tradition" as well as the "binding interpretation of Scripture by the church."[29] But while the dialogue commissions have dealt with these topics ever more intensively, they have not yet been able to establish that comprehensive agreement already exists concerning the central questions.

(6) The topics "the understanding Scripture" and "the use of Scripture" have already been the subjects of theological reflection many times *in the interna-*

---

basic principles of scriptural interpretation" in which the concern is "to recover the sense for the authority and obligatory nature of Sacred Scripture." Quotations are from the "Denver Report," no. 36, quoted in: H. Meyer, D. Papandreou, H. J. Urban, L. Vischer, eds., *Dokumente wachsender Übereinstimmung: Sämtliche Berichte und Konsenstexte interkonfessioneller Gespräche auf Weltebene*, vol. 1, Paderborn, Frankfurt 1983, second edition 1991, p. 396 [H. Meyer and L. Vischer, eds., *Growth in Agreement: Reports and Agreed Statements of Ecumenical Conversations on a World Level*, New York, Geneva 1984].

28 To justify its efforts to strive for the greatest possible agreement on the understanding of Scripture at the start of a dialogue, the commission of Evangelical Christians and the Roman Catholic Church states that "Roman Catholics and evangelicals will not come to close understanding or agreement on *any* topic if they cannot do so on *this* topic" ("Dialogue on Mission," quoted in: J. Gros, H. Meyer, and W. G. Rusch, eds., *Growth in Agreement II: Reports and Agreed Statements of Ecumenical Conversations on a World Level, 1982– 1998*, Grand Rapids, Michigan, Cambridge, Geneva 2000, p. 402).

29 Cf. for example the statements in the concluding report from 1977 on the dialogue between the World Alliance of Reformed Churches and the Secretariat for Promoting Christian Unity, "The Presence of Christ in Church and World," nos. 25–30, quoted in: H. Meyer et al., *Dokumente wachsender Übereinstimmung*, vol. 1 (note 27), p. 493f. Also see the report on the Baptist – Roman Catholic international conversations from 1984–1988, "Summons to Witness to Christ in Today's World," nos. 45–47, quoted in: J. Gros et al., *Growth in Agreement II* (note 28), p. 382f.

tional and national dialogues between the Protestant Churches and the Roman Catholic Church. In view of far-reaching agreement on the acceptance of the unity and normative nature of Holy Scripture for the faith and teaching of the church,[30] the efforts focused chiefly on questions concerning the relation of tradition to Scripture and the justification for and practice of the church's authoritative and binding interpretation of Scripture.

The document "The Gospel and the Church"[31], commonly known as the "Malta Report," formulated fundamental declarations on the relationship between Scripture and tradition, on the criteria for the proclamation of the church, and on the question of the center of Scripture. These statements were reinforced in later documents.[32] A continuation of the discussion followed in the dialogue between the Roman Catholic Church and the Lutheran Church both on the global level[33] and on the national level[34], especially with respect to the question of the binding nature of the interpretation of Scripture by the teaching office. Corresponding efforts to form a consensus in this thematic

---

30 Concerning this see in particular the document presented in 1980 by the Roman Catholic – Lutheran Joint Commission, "Ways to Community," nos. 62–65, quoted in: H. Meyer et al., *Dokumente wachsender Übereinstimmung*, vol. 1 (note 27), p. 310f.

31 Cf. "The Malta Report" ("The Gospel and the Church") of the Lutheran – Roman Catholic Joint Commission, 1972, nos. 14–25, quoted in: H. Meyer et al., *Dokumente wachsender Übereinstimmung*, vol. 1 (note 27), pp. 252–255.

32 Cf. "Facing Unity," 1984, no. 57, quoted in: J. Gros et al., *Growth in Agreement II* (note 28), p. 456f.; Lutheran – Roman Catholic Joint Commission, ed., *Church and Justification: Understanding the Church in the Light of the Doctrine of Justification*, Geneva 1994, no. 38, p. 30.

33 Cf. Roman Catholic – Lutheran Joint Commission, ed., *Das geistliche Amt in der Kirche*, Paderborn, Frankfurt 1981, pp. 39–42, nos. 50–58, also quoted in: H. Meyer et al., *Dokumente wachsender Übereinstimmung*, vol. 1 (note 27), pp. 346–348; Lutheran – Roman Catholic Joint Commission, ed., *Church and Justification* (note 32), nos. 205–222, pp. 100–108.

34 Cf. the Bilateral Study Group of the German Bishops' Conference and the Governing Body of the United Evangelical-Lutheran Church of Germany, *Kirchengemeinschaft in Wort und Sakrament*, Paderborn, Hannover 1984, nos. 75 and 76, pp. 84–90.

area can also be found in the texts documenting the dialogue between the World Alliance of Reformed Churches and the Roman Catholic Church.[35]

1.3 Our Efforts

(7) *The efforts of the Ecumenical Study Group* of Protestant and Catholic theologians to strengthen and to deepen what we hold in common with respect to our understanding of Holy Scripture and our description of exegetical criteria follow in the footsteps of the preceding endeavors. In the introduction to *The Condemnations of the Reformation Era: Do They Still Divide?* the study group already considered the "authority of Holy Scripture and its interpretation as foundation for an understanding of the beliefs disputed in the mutual condemnations" in detail.[36] The Ecumenical Study Group then initiated research on the fundamental question of the binding nature of biblical testimony for the teaching of the church. In 1992 it presented an important interim result of the deliberations in its joint statement on the topics "Canon – Holy Scripture – Tradition."[37]

The concluding report of the project "Binding Testimony" documented in the following text takes up, among other things, the issue identified in the introduction of *The Condemnations of the Reformation Era* as the remaining task of the ecumenical discussion, namely the problem that there is "as yet no explicit consensus about the critical function of Scripture with respect to the

---

35 Cf. "The Presence of Christ in Church and World," 1977, nos. 24–42, quoted in: H. Meyer et al., *Dokumente wachsender Übereinstimmung*, vol. 1 (note 27), pp. 493–497; "Towards a Common Understanding of the Church: Second Phase, 1984–1990," nos. 95–101, 121, 130–144, quoted in: H. Meyer et al., *Dokumente wachsender Übereinstimmung*, vol. 2 (note 28), p. 802f., p. 807, pp. 809–813.
36 Cf. K. Lehmann and W. Pannenberg, ed., *The Condemnations of the Reformation Era: Do They Still Divide?*, transl. by M. Kohl, Minneapolis 1990, pp. 24–28, quote p. 24, the heading to section III.
37 Cf. W. Pannenberg and Th. Schneider, ed., "Gemeinsame Erklärung," in: *Verbindliches Zeugnis I: Kanon – Schrift – Tradition*, Freiburg, Göttingen 1992, pp. 371–397. [This "Joint Statement" has been translated and is now part of the present book.]

church's formation of tradition."[38] Among the contrasting reactions *The Condemnations* experienced in the course of its reception[39] there were various responses supporting the Ecumenical Study Group's belief that a treatment of the fundamental question of the significance of Holy Scripture for the doctrinal traditions of the denominations is necessary. Individual comments on the first study expressed regret that the topic of "law and gospel" had not been treated in detail. The Ecumenical Study Group would also like to satisfy this desideratum in a new context.

(8) *In this document the Ecumenical Study Group directs its attention* in particular to the question of "the interpretation of Scripture." It attempts to reconcile or to mediate what are still widely felt to be conflicting positions: the "self-interpretation" of Scripture and the binding, "magisterial" interpretation of Scripture. The study begins, however, with reflections which document the agreement already achieved in the "understanding of Scripture."

Especially the challenge posed to a spiritual interpretation of Scripture by the historical-critical investigation of the Bible, but also initiatives from the Jewish-Christian dialogue make a joint effort to provide an answer to questions about the "unity" and "center" of the two biblical testaments seem appropriate.

The more recent exegetical and systematic-theological discussions of the methods of scriptural interpretation form the background for our effort. We want to take seriously the results produced by the historical investigation of Holy Scripture, but at the same time we want to achieve a shared understanding of Holy Scripture discerned exactly as it is in its historically developed verbal form as the word of the living God.

---

38 K. Lehmann and W. Pannenberg, ed., *The Condemnations of the Reformation Era* (note 1), p. 27.
39 Cf. W. Pannenberg and Th. Schneider, ed., *Lehrverurteilungen – kirchentrennend? IV. Antworten auf kirchliche Stellungnahmen*, Freiburg, Göttingen 1994 for a discussion of the questions formulated by Protestant and Roman Catholic committees concerning the results of the study *The Condemnations of the Reformation Era: Do They Still Divide?* (note 36).

2 Holy Scripture as the Word of God

2.1 Our Shared Confession

(9) The Christian churches confess together that God, the creator and supporter, has made Himself known as the God of life once and for all in Jesus Christ. God enlivens all His creatures through His Spirit; He frees all people from the clutches of sin and death and perfects all that is good which has its origin in Him.

God has revealed Himself in Jesus Christ and "made known to us ... the mystery of his will," namely His will for salvation which aims at "gather[ing] up all things in him [Christ], things in heaven and things on earth" (Eph 1:9f.). The choice of the people of Israel to whose ancestors God swore His covenant (cf. Deut 4:31) and to whom He told His name (cf. Ex 3:14; 34:6), belongs to the "economy" of God's salvific action which is directed towards this goal. In Jesus Christ God's will for salvation, which had been kept secret until then, is "disclosed" and made known to all nations through the writings of the prophets (cf. Rom 16:25f.). For their writings are inspired by God's Spirit (cf. 2 Tim 3:16) to witness to the fulfillment of His will for salvation in Jesus Christ. If God spoke to the ancestors "in many and various ways" (Heb 1:1), so He has now spoken to us in these last days by a Son.

(10) Hence it is understandable that right from the start the church not only respected the prophecy of the Old Testament scriptures as the very word of God, but also the apostolic preaching of Christ (cf. 1 Thess 2:13) and thus subsequently the scriptures of the New Testament as well. The scriptures of the Old and the New Testament have been written by human authors. The church, however, hears their words, the word of the Bible, as the word of God. This is especially clear in Christian liturgical services in the acclamations after the scriptural readings ("The word of the Lord" after the readings from the Old Testament and the epistles; "Glory to you, O Lord" and "Praise to you, Lord Jesus Christ" after the reading of the gospels), but also at the gospel procession with the alleluia in the Roman Catholic liturgy and the "little entrance" in the liturgy of the Orthodox Church. The triune God present in His word is being acclaimed. The constitutive significance of the

words of consecration for the Eucharist and of the command to baptize for baptism as well as the delegation of authority to forgive sins in absolution reflect this reality: Through His Spirit God Himself is the subject of the utterance and of the effect in each case, whereas the minister of the word stands, speaks, and acts in Christ's stead.

(11) Inasmuch as the individual biblical words and writings pertain to Jesus Christ, Holy Scripture as a whole is the word of the triune God and as such it is distinct in its authority, content and effect from every merely human word. The authority of Scripture as the word of God is closely connected to the theme of the unity of Scripture on the basis of its center. The original Christian scriptures thus cite the Old Testament as Holy Scripture in the Law and the Prophets, as a prophetic testimony to Jesus Christ through which God Himself has spoken. But Jesus Christ is the Word of God *per se* (cf. Jn 1:1) in which all of God's promises are fulfilled (cf. Rev 19:11–16; 2 Cor 1:20 and Heb 1:1f.). Hence the apostolic gospel as news about Jesus Christ is the word of God Himself and not just human words (cf. 1 Thess 2:13). As much as the apostolic proclamation is communicated by humans and in human language, it is still God's own word with respect to origin, authority and content. For this reason and as a result the scripture of the church, the Bible of the Old and the New Testament, is considered to be the word of God. It is the conclusive witness to the history of God with the world, to the selection of Israel, and to Jesus Christ as proclaimed by the apostolic gospel – with reference to the prophetic testimony about him.

2.2 Divine Inspiration

(12) Respect for the scriptures of the Old and the New Testament as the word of God has been common to all of Christianity since the early church. This has found expression in the *conviction that all of Scripture is divinely inspired*. Even in the controversy set off by the Reformation this conviction remained undisputed as such, although there was a conflict concerning responsibility for the interpretation of Scripture. *Sola scriptura* is not a neologism of the Reformation in every respect and it must not be misunderstood as a removal of Scripture from the process of the living transmission of the

gospel in the people of God. It is already contained *de facto* in the medieval placing of the authority of Scripture above all other forms of authority in the church. This involved appealing to Scripture as the permanently valid and effective means to distinguish the word of God from all human words in the church, which were supposedly necessary for salvation, and to reject the claims to validity raised for these. Distinctions were made, however, between the Scriptures of the Old Testament and those of the New Testament and between the different biblical authors. It was possible for such differentiation to lead to critical judgments about individual biblical writings even before the Reformation and particularly in the case of Luther, irrespective of the conviction that Scripture as a whole is the word of God. It is the word of God in its entirety from its center, from Jesus Christ. This provided Luther with the criterion for evaluating individual statements and parts of Scripture differently.

(13) *In early Protestant dogmatics* the post-Reformation controversy concerning *sola scriptura* and the principle of the clarity and self-interpretation of Scripture resulted in a further development of the traditional doctrine of inspiration in the sense of a divine authority and inerrancy which pertain equally to all scriptural passages. Here the oneness of the divine Spirit as the divine author of Scripture, who made use of the biblical authors as a means, was supposed to guarantee the contradiction-free agreement of all scriptural statements for the sake of the oneness of the teaching to be taken from Scripture. *The doctrine of verbal inspiration*, however, was not only developed in the theology of the Reformation. In the scholasticism of the Spanish baroque period Domingo Bañez (d. 1604) also taught the verbal inspiration of Scripture, and this view became the object of a controversy in Spain. In the 17th century verbal inspiration was adopted by Protestants as a rule due to its significance in the divisive theological disputes with Catholics. By means of this doctrine Scripture, as the sole source of church teaching, was to become independent of any reliance on a supplement in terms of content or on an authority of official interpretation other than itself.

(14) Unlike the Reformers' doctrine of Scripture, the early Protestant doctrine of Scripture as a foundation for church teaching which is uniform in itself, reliable in all details, and complete was vulnerable to any proof of human

imperfections in individual scriptural passages. Whereas the original teaching of the Reformation possessed the freedom to criticize individual biblical statements and entire canonical books by distinguishing between Scripture, the oral word of the gospel and Jesus Christ as the Word of God and center of Scripture, the later identification of the word of God and Scripture left no room for this. Every criticism of individual scriptural passages now had to be seen as immediately and fundamentally challenging the conviction that Scripture is the word of God. The corroboration of contradictions between particular scriptural statements, for instance in the case of biblical dates and times, and the discovery of conflicts between certain statements of Scripture and the newly acquired scientific knowledge of the world (as in Josh 10:12f.) thus shook the authority of Scripture *in toto* as the infallible word of God. The idea of an "accommodation" of the Holy Spirit as the author of Scripture to the humanly limited receptivity of the biblical authors as well as to each one's particular way of thinking and style did provide more room for taking the humanly conditioned nature of biblical statements into account when interpreting Scripture. At the same time, however, it undermined trust in Scripture as being the infallible word of God in all its statements. "Under the weight of the steadily growing number of insights with respect to the contingent nature of biblical statements as a result of their human-historical character, the Protestant theology of the 17th and 18th centuries could no longer adhere to the objective unity of Scripture's letter, spirit, and teaching which had been claimed in the early Protestant doctrine of Scripture."[40] Here the historical-critical researchers of biblical texts could refer to the conviction of the Reformation that there is an "external clarity" of Scripture for its central content by means of which Scripture itself is the criterion of its interpretation, in conjunction with the authoritativeness of the literal sense for interpretation (J. S. Semler). Historical-critical exegesis did not necessarily have to come into conflict with the view of Scripture as the word of God if the dogmatic doctrine of Scripture had left more room for the human-historical shape of biblical texts as had still been the case with the Reformation view of the relationship between God's word and Scripture.

---

40 *Verbindliches Zeugnis I* (note 37), p. 393 ["Joint Statement," part III, section 5 ("Frame of Reference for Contemporary Ecumenical Teaching on Scripture"), 5.3].

(15) Under the weight of the results of the historical-critical examination of biblical texts, theologians narrowed the view of Scripture as the word of God to its religious content being the word of God. As a result, corresponding to the newer development with respect to the understanding of inspiration in Catholic theology, the view that the word of God is contained in the human words of biblical writings replaced the identification of Scripture and word of God. This position, however, required an authority which would allow one to differentiate between the word of God and human words, and for Protestants this authority was increasingly assumed to lie in the religious subjectivity of the interpreter which would correspond to the religious subjectivity of the biblical authors themselves. Connected to this was the tendency to replace the subjective nature of the word of God with the human subjectivity present when Scripture was composed and is understood. Random events in the history of ideas and accidental convergences with one's own life experiences were able to achieve axiomatic status where one lost sight of the Christological criterion for the concept of the word of God, for its application to the apostolic gospel, and for the question concerning the connection between individual biblical statements and the totality of Scripture.

2.3 God's Word in Human Words

(16) There would only be a conflict between the notion of God's word in the human words of Scripture and the understanding of Scripture as the word of the triune God as it is heard and professed in the worship of the church if the humanness of the scriptural word were no longer recognized as a medium for the word of God which it witnesses to and makes present in an efficacious way. It is decisive for such recognition that the triune God is the subject in His word in which He discloses Himself and by which He is active in a judging and saving way. Through the words of Sacred Scripture the community is constituted and edified in its center, in its worship. Every interpretation of Sacred Scripture should serve the present acceptance of the message. Although the origin of Scripture in the historical past is the starting point for each interpretation of Scripture, its goal is the current use, the present acceptance of Scripture's message. It is interpreted and proclaimed because it is the

Sacred Scripture of the Christian community. The effect of Scripture in interpretation, proclamation and promise is also an essential part of its reality as the word of God. Where this is not seen and acknowledged one severs the exclusive connection between spirit and letter in the concept of Scripture as word of God.

(17) Correspondingly, when interpreting Scripture one should differentiate between *scholarly exegesis* and the interpretation of Scripture which occurs in the *doctrinal proclamation of the church*, while nevertheless acknowledging that they are connected to each other (see below, 8.5). The doctrinal proclamation of the church has the word of God in its current, proclaimed form as its object which is attested in Scripture and expressed anew today. The scholarly interpretation of Scripture must begin with the human-historical form of scriptural texts. Consequently it is initially bound to the literary sense of the text and is thus historical-critical exegesis. This is the only way one can understand the wording or language of biblical texts and assimilate it as such. For this reason scholarly exegesis is of fundamental importance for the doctrinal proclamation of the church. What is important for this proclamation, however, is not just the historical sense of the individual scriptural passages, but quite decisively God's words and deeds then and now which the individual biblical texts attest. For this proclamation needs to pay attention to the total witness of Scripture as it is revealed from its center in Jesus Christ. Such reference to the totality of Scripture is not necessarily out of reach of historical-critical exegesis; rather, shedding light on this totality is part of the task of biblical exegesis and should constitute its final goal. To approach this goal, however, exegetes must not only pay attention to the contexts of biblical writings and the connections among their parts, which should be reconstructed according to tradition-history, but also be open to the reality of God and His action in history which is witnessed to in these writings. This, however, involves questions and thematic aspects which go far beyond the specifically historical-critical task, but which influence the scope of judgments about what is historically possible. To exclude these is to limit the subject matter of biblical sayings to their human aspect, and so, for example, to see only the religious traditions of the people of Israel instead of God's actions towards them and only the early Christian Easter faith instead

of the resurrection of Jesus. An exegesis which is reduced to such an extent in its understanding of reality is only able to recognize human words in the biblical texts. It is then inevitable that the word of God in the human words becomes a matter for religious subjectivity to make an additional judgment about on the basis of faith. As a result the possible relevance of historical-critical exegesis for the scriptural interpretation of the church's doctrinal proclamation is restricted since this doctrinal proclamation must interpret the word of God given to the church in the testimony of Scripture as divine reality which precedes all religious subjectivity, is efficacious through the words of Scripture, and establishes the church.

(18) *The critical function of Scripture vis-à-vis the church* (see below, 8.5.2.2; 9.3.1.2; 9.5.3) is also part of the givenness of the word of God of Sacred Scripture prior to any interpretation by scholarly exegesis and church teaching. The question about establishing and restricting church authority is therefore connected to the recognition of Sacred Scripture as the word of God. The declaration of the Second Vatican Council that the "teaching office of the church is not above the word of God, but serves it" (*Dei Verbum* 10) establishes a point of departure for ecumenical agreement on this topic today. In this statement, however, the adherence to the word of Sacred Scripture is not expressed in a completely unequivocal manner since it says that the magisterium serves the word of God by teaching "only what has been handed on" (*Dei Verbum* 10). A further clarification of the relationship between Scripture and tradition is also necessary from the viewpoint of Catholic theology: The fidelity to what has been passed on *in Scripture* is decisive for the relationship between Scripture and the teaching office of the church. This unique authority of Scripture could also appear to be compromised through another formulation of the Council, namely through the statement that "it is not from sacred Scripture alone that the Church draws her certainty about everything which has been revealed" (*Dei Verbum* 9). Here, too, it must be shown that this statement of the Council does not entail any weakening of the authority of Scripture, but corresponds completely to the view of the Reformation that faith – which continually acquires certitude for the varied shape of its life over the course of time by looking at the original historical sense of scriptural statements – emerges originally and again and again from the *liv-*

ing proclamation of the gospel. It is the immediate source for faith's certitude about what has been revealed. The norm of Scripture alone, however, remains authoritative for the content of this proclamation (see below, 9.3.2.2).

(19) In accordance with what has been stated above about the relationship between ecclesial and scholarly interpretation of Scripture, the doctrinal proclamation of the church does not find its culmination in the historical and literary investigation of biblical texts, but must instead be subordinated to *the word of God* of Scripture which it serves. *Sola scriptura*, which is to be understood in the interest of the critical function of Scripture vis-à-vis church teaching, should not be placed in opposition to the living transmission of the gospel in the church, but appreciated as an expression of the normativeness of the biblical canon for the teaching of the church. The tradition of the church does indeed contribute to the interpreter's discerning more clearly what is contained in the wording of biblical texts. But the text itself, which is to be read within the context of the entire Bible, remains decisive as to whether this content is actually given in the biblical passage. The text is the foundation for the critical function of the word of God of Scripture vis-à-vis the doctrinal proclamation of the church. Although the historical-critical examination of the text plays a part here, it is not an exhaustive description of the critical function of the word of God. This function requires further clarification regarding the fidelity of church doctrinal proclamation to Jesus Christ as the incarnate word of God that is definitively witnessed by the apostolic gospel and given to all later ages of the church in the form of Sacred Scripture.

3 Worship as the Location Where God's Gospel Is Proclaimed

(20) The preaching of Jesus and the apostles lays the foundation for Christian worship – the liturgy of the different Christian churches – and determines it in an abiding way (cf. Lk 22,14–23; 1 Cor 11:23–26; Mt 28:19f.; Mk 16:15; Col 3:16). Sacred Scripture communicates this proclamation which for its

part, particularly in the sermon, strives to become oral and current (*viva vox*) ever anew.

3.1 The Connection between the Bible and the Liturgy

(21) The liturgy has held a central place in the life of the church from the beginning. This is especially true of the celebration of the sacraments. They make present for the individual and the entire faith community God's salvific action as witnessed in the Old and the New Testament. This is a decisive function of the worship of the church. Catechesis always leads to the liturgy, while mystagogical preaching – for its part a component of the liturgy – understands the latter reflectively. The encounter with God's gospel is at the center of the liturgy.

(22) *The presence of Scripture in the liturgy is multiform* and cannot be reduced to one formula. Among other things, this is a consequence of the different literary genera: reading, interpretation and preaching, song and prayer. Worship lives in the tension between personal participation and the communal celebration of God's salvific acts. Through the exalted Lord the individual believer and the celebrating community as a whole are placed in the history of faith of God's people of the old and the new covenant as well in the history of faith of the church, thus gaining a share in divine salvation.

(23) *The relationship between the Bible and liturgy has changed over the course of time* and acquired different forms in the different church traditions. The relationship between worship and preaching in particular was expressed in a great variety of ways in the course of history. The development of the modern book culture, i.e. the spread of books through the art of printing, played an especially important part since it meant that worship was no longer the exclusive place for encountering the biblical message. Nevertheless, the distinctiveness of the way the liturgy deals with Scripture has remained. What is proper to or special about the use of Scripture in worship is that Sacred Scripture is not only read and interpreted in the liturgy, but also celebrated. The gospel of Sacred Scripture acquires its doxological character in the liturgy with its verbal and non-verbal actions.

(24) *The close relationship between the Bible and liturgy can also be construed from the developments of the 20th century.* In Protestantism as well as Catholicism a major renewal movement after the First World War affected the Bible and the liturgy in like manner. The current crisis of the churches in central European societies involves both the understanding of the Bible as authoritative, divine instruction for one's life and the understanding of the liturgy as an actualization of the divine bestowal of salvation.

3.2 The Relationship between Faith and Celebration

(25) The liturgies of the churches of the East and West have always lived from their relationship with Scripture. And yet the relationship between Scripture and liturgy is multilayered. On the one hand the criterion for proper Christian worship is its conformity to Scripture; on the other hand the use of scriptures in the liturgy was the criterion for their acceptance as Holy Scripture. Worship is *a testimony of faith in the unity of Scripture* and at the same time a constitutive element of this faith. The worship of the church makes it possible to view the events of salvation as a whole. In this total view the canon of the Old Testament writings remains open to the further salvation history and its testimony in the New Testament writings. Precisely for this reason the testimony to God's salvific action through Jesus Christ remains of necessity dependent on the witness of the Old Testament.[41]

(26) From a historical perspective the unity of Scripture has been sustained through the *interpretatio christiana* (cf. 2 Cor 3:6–18) of the Old Testament which for early Christians was the Bible *per se*. This use of the Old Testament which was established in the New Testament has recently been under more intense discussion. Our task today is to see the idea of the unity of Scripture, substantiated and concretized through the reference to Jesus Christ, while at the same time recognizing the significance of the Old Testament writings in and of themselves (see below, 4 and 5).

---

41 Cf. *Verbindliches Zeugnis I* (note 37), p. 384 ["Joint Statement," part II, section 5 ("Conclusions"), 5.2].

(27) When considering the relationship between Christian worship and the biblical scriptures in a systematic way we should take account of the historical fact that, although people read from Holy Scripture in the Christian liturgy in the first centuries, the biblical canon and the liturgical form of celebration were still part of oral tradition to a great extent. The *official standardization of the liturgy* came after the final *determination of the biblical canon*. This standardization, however, did not necessarily serve the dynamic transmission of the word of Scripture. It is true that biblical readings and hymns continued to be read and sung, but the latter were increasingly replaced by non-biblical poetry and in some cases by literature which had nothing to do with the Bible. The presence of Scripture in the liturgy lost its effectiveness in particular in places where the language of the liturgy no longer corresponded to the language of the faithful and where, moreover, the majority of the faithful could not read. As a result the corrective function of biblical proclamation was increasingly absent from the church's practice of faith unless the faithful found some substitute in non-liturgical forms of biblical instruction, such as the "picture bibles" depicted on church windows and in portal sculptures, the kind of popular preaching that had flourished since the 12th century, and within the framework of the new forms of pastoral care provided by the new religious orders since the 13th century.

(28) Systematic theology, however, always kept an eye on the reciprocal relationship between the Bible and liturgy, especially in the context of the sacraments; but due to the above-mentioned language barrier its expositions rarely spread to liturgical practice. Although the diversity of the relationship of liturgy to Scripture continued to be handed down in the different liturgical forms which were used, it could no longer be discerned by the faithful and remained lost to the life of faith to a large extent. In the Protestant church the Reformation opened the door wide to a spiritual renewal of the relationship between the Bible and liturgy. In the Catholic church it was in particular the liturgical reform of the Second Vatican Council that expanded and intensified the reading and interpretation of Scripture in worship.

4 The Unity and Totality of Holy Scripture

(29) To read the Bible as a canon of inspired writings means to see it in its *totality* as an *integrated whole* which is clearly defined theologically. We can speak of the "unity" of Scripture if the *one* word of the *one* God is heard in the different human witnesses through the *one* Spirit; we can speak of its "totality" if this hearing of the word of God requires that *all* the texts and all the theological positions discernible in them have their say. The material sufficiency of Scripture, which Protestant and Catholic theology agree upon,[42] presupposes its theological coherence. Without the discernment of its unity and totality the binding nature of the biblical witness cannot be made apparent either in the interpretation of Scripture or in the church's practice of faith as a whole.

4.1 The Task

(30) In the history of the Christian understanding and use of Scripture what comprises the unity of *all* of Holy Scripture and how it can be recognized has been variously interpreted. Denominational differences played a major role in the past, and they have not completely disappeared in the present. At the moment, however, they have been eclipsed by fundamental questions concerning the genuinely Christian understanding of Scripture which do not stem from the divisive theological discussions between the denominations. The historical-critical investigation of Holy Scripture, being oriented towards

---

42 Cf. *Verbindliches Zeugnis I* (note 37), p. 385f. ["Joint Statement," part III, section 1 ("Ecumenical Convergences"), 1.1]. Our interpretation of the decree of the Council of Trent on the "Reception of the Sacred Books and Apostolic Traditions," DH 1501 [ND 210], and of *Dei Verbum* 9–11 is corroborated in the statements on the "Relationship between Tradition and Sacred Scripture" in the *Catechism of the Catholic Church* (pars. 80–83), especially by the differentiation made in no. 83 concerning the concept of tradition which partially converges in substance with our clarification of this concept as found in the *Augsburg Confession*; cf. *Verbindliches Zeugnis I* (note 37), pp. 386–388 ["Joint Statement," part III, section 1 ("Ecumenical Convergences"), 1.2].

the original historical sense of the biblical texts, has made us more keenly aware than before of the difference between the "theologies" of the two testaments and aware of the plurality and in some cases contradictory nature of the theological positions within Holy Scripture. In addition, the traditional *interpretatio Christiana* of the Old Testament has become a problem in the context of Jewish-Christian dialogue.

(31) The challenge facing theology and the church is to use these critical questions for the benefit of a new reflection on the unity of Scripture. It is of particular importance to see the duality of the testaments and the variety of biblical texts in their positive relationship to the unity and totality of Scripture. These issues have barely been resolved yet in contemporary Christian theology, although they are being addressed by some very promising approaches.

(32) *On the one hand* the task consists in developing a Christian understanding of the Old Testament that rediscovers its theological relevance without disregarding its significance for the Jews and without relativizing the Christ event.

On the other hand the task consists in perceiving the diversity of the Bible as an expression of its theological wealth without diminishing the importance of the canon itself and without dispensing with evaluations within the Old and the New Testament.

These tasks can only be accomplished if theological efforts can clarify that the results correspond to the witness of Scripture itself and are convincing within the context of present-day appreciation of truth and awareness of problems. On this condition we can ask anew whether the differences between the denominational traditions of scriptural interpretation really have a church-dividing character or whether they instead could contribute to the enrichment of an ecumenically binding understanding and use of Scripture.

4.2 The Profession of the Oneness of God and the Unity of Scripture

(33) The unity of Scripture follows from the "oneness" of God which both Israel and the church profess (cf. Deut 6:4f.; Mk 12:32f.). Seeing the Sacred Scripture of the Old and the New Testament as a connected unity conforms to the witness of the Bible itself. But at the same time it corresponds to the continuity of church tradition which was never challenged in the denominational controversies during the time of the Reformation.[43] Seeing Scripture as a unity is a consequence of professing the triune God – according to Scripture –[44]

- as the Father, the Creator of the world (cf. Gen 1; Ps 104 and 148) who called the patriarchs (cf. Gen 12) and chose Israel as His people in fidelity to His promises (cf. Deut 4 and 7; Rom 9:6, 11:29; Heb 11), who "spoke to our ancestors in many and various ways by the prophets, but in these last days ... has spoken to us by a Son" (Heb 1:1f.), and who will create "new heavens and a new earth" (Isa 65:17, 66:22; 2 Pet 3:13; Rev 21:1) so that God may be "all in all" (1 Cor 15:28);
- as the Son, the incarnate Word of God (cf. Jn 1:1–18), the mediator of creation (cf. Jn 1:3; 1 Cor 8:6; Col 1:16; Heb 1:2), who, having been sent by the Father, is one with the Father (cf. Jn 10:30), who in his death on the cross and in his resurrection "takes away the sin of the world" (Jn 1:29), and who has thus become to all who believe in him "the source of eternal salvation" (Heb 5:9; cf. Rom 3:21–26);
- as the Holy Spirit, who, creating (cf. Gen 2:7; Ps 33:6) and re-creating (cf. Ezek 37:1–14; 1 Cor 15:45–50), purifying and sanctifying (cf. Isa 32:15–2)

---

43 Cf. Luther's prefaces to the "entire" Holy Scripture, especially to the Old Testament in: M. Luther, *Werke. Kritische Gesamtausgabe* ("Weimarer Ausgabe"), Weimar, 1883ff., *Deutsche Bibel* 8,10–32, Calvin's *Institutes of the Christian Religion*, I.7.1, and the decree of the Council of Trent on the "Reception of the Sacred Books and Apostolic Traditions," DH 1501 [ND 210].

44 With respect to the following Trinitarian approach cf. both the first thesis of the Barmer Theological Statement in: W. Niesel, ed., *Bekenntnisschriften und Kirchenordnungen der nach Gottes Willen reformierten Kirchen*, Zurich, 2nd edition, 1938 and the first chapter of *Dei Verbum*, "Divine Revelation Itself".

and differentiating and inspiring (cf. Isa 61:1–11; Lk 4:18f.; Acts 1:5; 1 Cor 12:4–11), not only effects the salvific presence of God in the world of humans He created (cf. Job 33:4; Jn 3:8; Rom 5:5) while causing His creatures at the same time to open themselves to Him (cf. Ezek 11:19, 36:26f.; Jn 4:23f.; Gal 4:6f.; Rom 8:15, 26f.), but in the course of this also joins the faithful from Israel and from all nations together into God's eschatological community of salvation (cf. Isa 42:1–4; Joel 3:1–5 [Joel 2:28–32 in the NRSV]; Acts 2:38f.; Rom 8:11; Eph 2:18–22).

This triune God is the one, unique, only true God. He remains faithful to His promises; He makes Himself known in His saving will "through humans in human fashion" (Augustine, *The City of God*, XVII, 6,2) so that He can be acknowledged and professed as the "living and true God" (1 Thess 1:9). This is the foundation for the unity of the Sacred Scriptures of the Old and the New Testament.

(34) With the profession of the oneness of God, the testimony of Scripture rejects all attempts to deny the unity of Scripture by referring to the tensions between the two testaments or to the theological differences between Old Testament and New Testament texts. At the same time, with the biblically grounded knowledge of faith about the historicity of the revelatory action of God, it rejects all attempts to deny the plurality of Old and New Testament theologies or the tension between the two testaments by invoking the oneness of the Spirit and the Christocentricity of the eschatological salvation event. The Bible grounds the conviction of faith that precisely in this tension between the two testaments and in the diversity of their theological conceptions the *one* word of God can be heard which establishes the unity of all of Sacred Scripture.

(35) Since the unity of Scripture is grounded in the oneness of God, it cannot be found in the identity or the complementarity of the theological positions assumed in it. What is decisive instead is that the biblical writings are oriented to "the God of Abraham, the God of Isaac, and the God of Jacob" (Ex 3:6; Mk 12:26) throughout and attest His judging, and even more His saving action. Through Jesus Christ and through the power of the Holy Spirit God's action extends from the creation of the world to the final establishment of the

kingdom of God; hence it manifests itself first of all in the election of the people of Israel (cf. Deut 7:6f.; Rom 9:1–4) in order to pass on the blessing of Abraham (cf. Gen 12:2) to all nations (cf. Mt 1:1, 28:16–20; Gal 3:6–14; Rom 4:23–25) in "the fullness of time" (Gal 4:4) through the sending, the work, the death and the raising of Jesus. For the sake of the *Deus semper major* this biblical gospel demands a great variety of themes, positions and perspectives of biblical theologies which is as far from being nonobligatory and arbitrary as it is from being monotonous and uniform. And because of God's salvation-oriented will to have his kingdom come near (cf. Mk 1:15) and to send His Son (cf. Gal 4:4) in the fullness of time, the biblical gospel requires both the precise distinction and the fundamental connection between the Old Testament and the New Testament witness of faith.

5 The Two Testaments in the One Holy Scripture

(36) It is only within the framework of the Christ event that the question concerning the theological unity of the Old and the New Testament is posed. Therefore it can also only be answered within this framework: on the condition that it is Jesus the Son of God – who is preexisting and incarnate, who acted with authority, died for many, was raised from the dead on the third day, was glorified, and will come again to judge the living and the dead – through whom God the Father realizes His kingdom. But precisely on this condition a threefold task faces presents itself because the God of Jesus is the God of Israel:

- We have to consider what canonical significance the Old Testament – the historical witness to the *one* God who in His revelatory action showed Himself to be the God of all life and the one who chose Israel (cf. Ex 20:2 and 34:6f.) – has for *Christians*.
- We must shed light on what the canonical significance of the New Testament is – the witness to the Christ event as the *ultimate* saving action of this one God.
- And finally on this foundation we have to determine how the two testaments relate to each other in the *one* Bible.

5.1 The Significance of the Old Testament

(37) Protestant and Catholic Christians both read the Old Testament as God's binding word. In their histories both groups are familiar with the temptation to reject or at least to suppress the Old Testament. But if they do not give in to this temptation, both can find orientation in important texts of their shared tradition[45] as well as in those of their respective, denominationally specific traditions[46]. At the same time and above all else they stand in the tradition of Jesus (cf. Mk 12:28–34) and the early church (cf. Mk 12:36; Rom 1:2f.; 2 Tim 3:15–17; 2 Pet 1:19–21), both of which adopted the Old Testament and the early Jewish understanding of canonicity[47] and inspiration[48] in their own understanding of the "holy scriptures" (Rom1:2) as the word of God.

(38) In the New Testament and in the early church the Old Testament primarily served to characterize words and deeds, but also the suffering and raising of Jesus, as salvation events in terms of the promises of Scripture (cf. 1 Cor 15:3–5; Jn 12:13–17). Corresponding to this, but conversely, the Old Testament was read and interpreted in the light of the Christ event.[49] In the traditional method of interpretation of the multiple or fourfold sense of Scripture, the specific importance of the Old Testament, insofar as it documents Israel's history of faith, is acknowledged by means of the "literal" sense. The "allegorical" sense of Scripture tries to derive the deeper, salvific

---

45 The clearest document is the canon itself which consists in a constitutive way of the Old *and* the New Testament.
46 Cf. for instance on the one hand Luther's prefaces to the Old Testament in: M. Luther, *Werke* (note 43), to the Psalter in: idem, 10/I, 98–105, and to the Prophets in: idem, 11/I, 2–15, as well as Calvin's *Institutes of the Christian Religion*, I.7; on the other hand cf. the decree of the Council of Trent on the "Reception of the Sacred Books and Apostolic Traditions," DH 1501 [ND 210].
47 Cf. Deut 4:2, 13:1, 30:15–20; Eccl 3:14; Jer 26:2; Prov 30:6; SirProl; *Letter of Aristeas*, 311.
48 Cf. Isa 61:1f.; 2 Esd 14:38–44; Philo, *Vita Mosis*, 2, 188; Josephus, *Against Apion*, 1, 36f.
49 This reading of the Old Testament occurs in a very pronounced way in Paul, Matthew, John and Hebrews (in each case differently).

significance of Old Testament passages by starting from and moving toward Jesus.

(39) Seen from today's perspective, the *interpretatio Christiana* must be viewed with greater discrimination.

From a historical perspective it created a fundamental precondition for the possibility of establishing the legitimacy and the plausibility of the apostolic gospel. Then *interpretatio Christiana* was (in Irenaeus and Origen) an argument against both the Marcionite rejection and the Gnostic reinterpretation of the Old Testament. In theological terms it addresses a surplus of meaning in Old Testament texts which is not manifest in the original literal sense, but becomes clear from the perspective of the Christ event and which can be fruitful in a hermeneutics of the whole Bible. This is the case because the awareness of God's action as it is related in the New Testament since the historical coming of Jesus Christ is deepened, supplemented and enriched by the awareness of the same God's action as it is attested in the Old Testament from the time before the incarnation of Jesus Christ – just as, conversely, the witness to God given in the Old Testament is supplemented, enriched, deepened and opened up in a new way by the witness to God encountered in the New Testament as a result of the Christ event. The New Testament also always shows who God is in view of the Old, and the Old Testament also always in view of the New.

(40) Still we cannot ignore the fact that in the case of very many, even central texts considerable tensions have emerged with respect to both traditional Jewish interpretations and historical-critical interpretations of the Old Testament. The profound differences between a Jewish interpretation and a Christian interpretation of the same scriptures should be acknowledged on a theological level and utilized for a Christian understanding of Scripture which has been renewed from its sources. Offensive anti-Jewish remarks by some even prominent interpreters of Scripture present a special problem which must be faced critically, especially where these interpreters cite the stereotypical criticism of the "pharisees" or "the Jews" in some New Testament texts. The anti-Jewish statements of Christian exegetes of Scripture, which are in no way connected to the approach of the *interpretatio Christiana* or

the doctrine of the multiple sense of Scripture as such, but at most represent questionable applications of these, must be overcome by Scripture itself in the tension and unity it displays between the Old and the New Testament.

(41) The recognition of the sometimes radical difference between a traditional *interpretatio Christiana* and the original historical sense of Old Testament texts also affords us Christians the opportunity to acquire a new approach to the significance of the Old Testament. This significance of the Old Testament is that it presents God as the creator and sustainer of the world, as the judge and the merciful rescuer, and as the Lord of history who has entered into an everlasting covenant of grace with Israel to which He steadfastly adheres, and who gives His chosen people, and thereby all peoples, the great promise of life which, according to more recent scriptural texts, will not be fulfilled until the kingdom of God comes. The further significance of the Old Testament for Christians, which is inseparably connected to these basic theological positions in the message about God the creator, sustainer and Lord of history, consists in giving them instructions for the concrete conduct of their lives before God with the Decalogue and also with a vast number of other texts. The Old Testament also gives their prayers a voice, in particular with the psalter. For these reasons the Old Testament forms the first part of the Christian canon, not only as a preparation for the revelation of Christ, but also in its own theological and historical right. Even in the light of the Christ event it remains the fundamental witness to Israel's history of faith. Since it is the one Lord (cf. Deut 6:4f.) who has acted in Israel's history for His people and spoken to them in a variety of ways and the same God who, according to our faith, has spoken and acted in His Son Jesus Christ to save Israel and all the nations, the Old Testament belongs to the Bible of Christians in an absolutely essential way.

(42) The remaining differences between Protestant and Catholic teaching with respect to determining the extent of the Old Testament canon do not touch the core of the shared, basic understanding of the Holy Scripture of the

Old Testament.[50] The early church kept to the Old Testament in the dimensions of the Septuagint scriptures. Catholics acknowledge that the questionable books do not have a "protocanonical", but a "deuterocanonical" character in view of the particular history of their origin and transmission. Protestants today see the significance of the so-called "Apocrypha" not least of all against the backdrop of biblical scholarship which emphasizes the importance of the Septuagint writings and early Judaism for the formation of New Testament theology. Lutherans, moreover, can cite Luther's judgment that these books are "good and helpful to read."

The Ecumenical Study Group repeats its suggestion[51] that in *editions of the Bible* one should proceed in the way designated by the "Guidelines for Interconfessional Cooperation in Translating the Bible" (1987): The "deuterocanonical" (or "apocryphal") books are printed in their own block before the New Testament texts.[52]

(43) In the churches of the Reformation the "deuterocanonical" books (the so-called "Apocrypha") are not intended for use as lessons in worship or texts for sermons. In the Roman Catholic church, however, the Old Testament reading is occasionally taken from these "deuterocanonical" scriptures. These divergent practices reflect the denominational differences in the determination of the size of the Old Testament canon. Nevertheless, both sides can be sure that their reasons are respected which, on the one hand, result in the Roman Catholic church taking the "deuterocanonical" (or "apocryphal") books into account occasionally in its lectionary and, on the other hand, lead the Protestant churches to disregard them in their lectionaries. In any case, this difference between the Protestant and the Roman Catholic lectionary traditions does not have a divisive character for the churches.

---

50 Regarding this cf. "Gemeinsame Erklärung," in: *Verbindliches Zeugnis I* (note 37), pp. 371–397 [This is the entire text of the "Joint Statement" which is printed in English as part of the present book].
51 Cf. ibid., p. 384 ["Joint Statement," part II, section 5 ("Conclusions"), 5.3].
52 "Moreover, these guidelines prefer to use the designation 'deuterocanonical' rather than the word 'apocryphal' which is used in a different sense and is thus ambiguous." (ibid.)

5.2 The Significance of the New Testament

(44) The authors of the scriptures of the New Testament make it clear that the gospel of Jesus Christ[53] as the gospel of God[54] possesses[55] a sweeping claim to being true and binding. Christians affirm this claim to authority since it is the glorified Christ himself who witnesses to himself in the gospel through the power of the Spirit (cf. 1 Cor 2:3–5; 2 Cor 5:11, 6:10; Rom 10:14–17; Rev 1:9f.). He did this initially in all the forms of oral proclamation in the worship and teaching of the early church. But the positive significance attached to the written form for its reliable and binding proclamation of the gospel is already reflected in some passages of the New Testament (Jn 20:30f.; Rev 22:18f.; cf. 2 Cor 10:10f.; Rom 15:15).

(45) The significance of the New Testament lies above all in its testimony to Jesus Christ who was mortal as well as raised from the dead, crucified as well as glorified, and is preexisting, but will also come again for the final judgment. At the same time this witness to Christ is, in all its dimensions, *theo*-logy: proclamation of the *one* God who reveals Himself in the fullness of His grace through Jesus Christ. Precisely this theocentrism is the condition which also makes New Testament Christology always be soteriology: speech about the radical dependency of sinful people on God's mercy and about the possibility of the forgiveness of sins, mercifully granted to the believers, and of ultimate salvation through Jesus Christ. The ecclesiological and ethical positions of the New Testament are also understood from these theological relationships. The *ecclesia* composed of Jews and Gentiles is the "body in Christ" (Rom 12:5) inasmuch as it has been constituted through the crucified one who has been raised. Ethics is understood as expressing a binding acceptance of the gospel that has been proven in social relationships. For its part this acceptance consists in the Spirit-wrought participation in the love of God through Jesus Christ (cf. Rom 5:5; 1 Cor 13; 1 Jn 4:7–16).

---

53 Cf. Mk 1:1; Rom 15:19; 1 Cor 9:12, 2 Cor 2:12; Gal 1:7.
54 Cf. Rom 15:16; 2 Cor 11:4; 1 Pet 4:17; cf. Mk 1:14; Acts 20:24.
55 Cf. Mt 1:1; Lk 1:1–4; Mk 1:1; Jn 20:30f., 21:24; 1 Thess 2:13; Heb 5:11–6:3; Rev 22:18f.

(46) The normative significance of the New Testament is not relativized, but strengthened instead by the fact that we can already read fundamental, permanently valid statements in the Old Testament about God and about humans. Conversely, Jesus does not readily confirm the messianic expectations which had been developed – in a very multifaceted manner – in the Old Testament and in early Judaism. He is "the messiah of God" (Lk 9:20; cf. Acts 2:36, 3:18) in his very own, incredibly new way – and *for this reason* he is the fulfillment of God's promises in person for early Christianity. Consequently both Jesus' proclamation of God and that of the New Testament authors are not simply rooted in Old Testament and early Jewish proclamation, but also contain essentially new features since God is no longer simply addressed as Father of the patriarchs (cf. personal names like Abraham and Joab), Father of the king (cf. 2 Sam 7:14; Ps 2:7) or Father of all people (Mal 2:10), but as Father of Jesus (cf. Mk 14:36), and in this respect as Father of all who believe in Jesus (cf. Mt 6:9–13, par. Lk 11:1–4; Jn 14; Gal 4:6; Rom 8:15). Furthermore, from this it follows that from the perspective of the New Testament it is not only possible to say with important Old Testament witnesses (cf. Ps 103; Isa 43:1–7; Hos 14:2–9) that the hoped-for salvation can only happen by the grace of God; rather, it must likewise be emphasized that precisely for this reason salvation takes place through Jesus Christ alone (cf. Gal 2:16–21; Jn 1:17f.). And finally, it also follows that the relationship to one's neighbor (cf. Lev 19:18) is not only determined by the relationship to the *one* God who also gives His love to the "stranger" (cf. Deut 10:18f.; Lev 19:34); rather, Christian ethics is determined in its theocentrism by the relationship to Jesus Christ who died "for many" (Mk 14:24), in particular for the sinners (cf. Rom 5:8) and above all for the "enemies" of God (Rom 5:10).

5.3 The Tension-filled Unity of the Old and the New Testament

(47) The Old and the New Testament belong together in the Christian Bible. Their connection is tension-filled, but inseparable and reciprocal. This connection can be properly understood only if one bears in mind that what are linked are not just two text complexes, but the Old Testament and the New Testament witnesses to God's revelatory action in history.

A constructive examination of those hermeneutical models which have been developed in the history of the church is an appropriate approach for understanding this relationship.

5.3.1 Models of Interpretation in History

The reciprocal relationship between the two testaments has been described in different ways throughout the centuries. The models correspond to the hermeneutical premises of their respective periods. We must reconsider them in the context of current problems and use them for the benefit of our discussion.

(48) Central passages in the New Testament (especially in Matthew, Luke, John and Paul, but also in the First Letter of Peter and in Hebrews) already consider the relationship between God's salvific action for Israel as it is attested in Old Testament scripture and the Christ event under the categories of *promise and fulfillment*. This definition of the relationship had a particularly powerful impact as far back as the patristic period, but also in scholasticism and the Reformation.

Originally it did not in any way aim at an appropriation of (Old Testament) "Scripture" by the Christians, as is occasionally presumed today – even if Christian theology did not remain immune to such temptations during its history. On the contrary, what is decisive is the profession of faith that on the one hand the Christological salvation event occurred "in accordance with the scriptures" (1 Cor 15:3–5) and that on the other hand the salvific work of Jesus Christ eschatologically realizes (cf. 2 Cor 1:20) the salvific action of God for Israel as it is witnessed in the "law and prophets" (cf. Mt 5:17–20). This realization is primarily the realization of the kingdom of God perfected in the future which, however, is anticipated at present "in Christ," to use the language of St. Paul.

(49) The historical-critical interpretation of the Old Testament contributes to exposing the problems with this hermeneutical model of promise and fulfillment since it demonstrates the considerable differences in many cases between the original sense of the texts (as far as this can be reconstructed) and

their reception in the New Testament. For the sake of a biblical theology which wants to detect the richness of Scripture while taking into account present-day awareness of methods, the discrepancy between the original sense and the reception must not be harmonized after the fact. But one should also bear in mind that reception-critical research, as it has recently been done intensively in biblical studies, cautions against fixing an interpretation to a single original historical sense; it calls attention instead to the living processes of tradition which run their course within the Bible and also between the two testaments. This viewpoint provides a new exegetical approach to the old relational model of promise and fulfillment.

(50) This approach is predicated on an awareness of two perspectives: The first is the path of God which covers a long period of time and is attested in Scripture, and the second is the eschatological theocentrism in which the New Testament conceptions of the Christological fulfillment of Scripture are ultimately rooted. On the condition that these perspectives are taken into consideration, the witness of the Old Testament scriptures is not judged solely by its prognostic quality, nor is the witness of the New Testament scriptures limited to the conceptual framework of Old Testament theology. Rather, from the perspective of eschatological theocentrism the correlation of "promise" and "fulfillment" acquires a dynamic which embraces the entire Bible and which, in its soteriological finality, can show those searching for the unity of the Old and the New Testament important paths to follow.

(51) A different model for determining the relationship between the two testaments which is likewise laid out in the New Testament (cf. 1 Cor 10:1–13; Gal 4:21–31; Heb 7–9; 1 Pet 3:21) is the model of *typology*.[56] Examples of this include understanding an Old Testament event as a prefiguration of a New Testament event in which it is completely realized; or understanding a New Testament occurrence as outdoing and fulfilling an Old Testament occurrence; or describing a New Testament fact in accordance with an Old Testament fact. In the New Testament, in the patristic period, as well as during the Middle Ages and the early Modern Era, typological thinking presup-

---

56 Typological thinking is already present in the Old Testament as well, e.g. in speech about the "new Exodus" or the "new heaven and the new earth."

posed the continuity of the salvific action of God, while reflecting at the same time on the eschatological consummation which is realized through Jesus Christ. This theology of the Bible is expressed in a particularly significant way in a statement Augustine made: "*Novum in Vetere latet et in Novo Vetus patet*" ["The New is hidden in the Old and the Old is made manifest in the New"] (*Quaestiones in Heptateuchum*, 2.73).[57]

(52) The critical objections to the typological model, which were raised as a result of the impact of historical research, are similar to those expressed in the case of the closely related model of promise and fulfillment: The Old Testament texts and the reality they describe are accorded significance solely in a derivative and provisional sense which is only apparent from the perspective of the New Testament. Nonetheless, the fact that God's path and analogies of His action are subsequently recognized, formulated, attested, and extolled definitely conforms to the results of an inner-biblical development of tradition. We should appreciate typological exegesis in view of such retrospectively discerned analogies of God's action for two reasons. On the one hand, more recent biblical research is discovering a wealth of structural analogies between the theological witnesses of both testaments and is thus taking up an important theme of typological exegesis. These analogies appear during the course of the entire history of God with the world. The biblical texts concentrate and consolidate the historical events in this overall history. On the other hand, contemporary ideas about the relationship between the Old and the New Testament must also confront questions addressed by typological hermeneutics regarding the unity of the biblical history of revelation and the new eschatological orientation of soteriology through the Christology of the New Testament.

---

57 This theology is reflected in Martin Luther's "Church Postil" of 1522: "... (T)he New Testament is nothing other than a revelation of the Old, just as if someone first had a sealed letter and then opened it," in: M. Luther, *Werke* (note 43), 10/I, 1, 181,24 – 182,1. It is quoted in Roman Catholic documents time and again (the last time in *Dei Verbum* 16 and in the 1993 *Catechism of the Catholic Church*, no. 129). The model of typology corresponds to the scriptural theology of the Reformed churches to a lesser degree; this theology looks more intensely at structural analogies between the history of Israel and the church within the framework of the one history of salvation.

(53) Particularly in the Gospel of Luke and in Acts we encounter the theological view that God's actions in the history of Israel, in the history of Jesus and in the history of the church are to be understood in the context of *salvation history* which is wrought by the Spirit. This salvation-historical way of thinking must definitely not ignore the eschatological caesura which the coming of Jesus Christ represents (cf. Mk 1:1–15; Jn 1:1–18; Gal 4:4; Heb 1:1–4). In the later history of theology this approach also led to all sorts of harmonizations between the theological statements of the two testaments. It does, however, provide a hermeneutical key for grasping the *theocentric* coherence of the biblical history of revelation: the unity of history based on God's faithfulness to His promises. And last, but not least, theocentric coherence in this form has shaped the Roman Catholic understanding of Scripture as expressed most recently in *Dei Verbum* 3–6.

(54) Since John Calvin (*Institutes of the Christian Religion*, II.9–11) Reformed theology has understood the unity of Scripture in the duality of its testaments in terms of the *concept of covenant*. Calvin stresses the unity of the covenant emphatically. He sees the covenant constituted throughout by the "hope for immortality," by its foundation "in the mercy of God" and by the mediation of Jesus Christ (*Institutes of the Christian Religion*, II.10.2 in the context of 9–12). This covenant theology has great ecumenical potential: It does, after all, go back to central texts of the Old and the New Testament in order to find a comprehensive concept for the entire salvation event attested in the Bible, a concept which, in the end, it always considers in the correlation of the reign of God and the people of God. Of course it cannot be overlooked that both Old Testament and New Testament research has arrived at differentiated evaluations and interpretations of biblical covenant theology or theologies and that, although the Christocentric interpretation of the *one* covenant of God appears consistent from a New Testament perspective, there is tension between it and the original historical meaning of the relevant Old Testament texts. Therefore the determination of the relationship between the two parts of Scripture in terms of covenant theology must also be reconsidered from the perspective of Scripture itself.

(55) In some powerful currents of Lutheran theology the view has been developed that the relationship between the two testaments should be under-

stood as that of *law and gospel*: Whereas one should hear the word of God through the Old Testament scriptures above all as a law of judgment which makes the greatness of one's guilt due to sin clear to a person and points out the impossibility of saving oneself, one encounters the word of God in the New Testament above all as a gospel which forgives sins and justifies the believer by grace alone. Over against this perception it must of course be asserted that, although Martin Luther, who called the correct distinction between law and gospel the heart of all theology (cf. *Werke. Kritische Gesamtausgabe* {"Weimarer Ausgabe"}, Weimar, 1883ff., 7, 502,34f.; 36, 9,26–29; 40/I, 207,3ff.), saw the judging law as predominate in the Old Testament and the gospel of promise as predominate in the New Testament, he by no means identified the "law" with the Old Testament and the "gospel" with the New Testament. Instead, when considering its effect on the hearer he applied "law" and "gospel" in a dialectical way to the word of God of Old and New Testament Scripture as a whole (see below, 7).

5.3.2 Foundations of a Contemporary, Ecumenical Definition of the Relationship

(56) From a contemporary point of view, we can only succeed in defining the relationship between the two testaments in the context of the *one* Holy Scripture by duly appreciating both the discussions in the history of theology and exegetical research. Two key points need to be stressed in particular.

(57) *First*, the New Testament absolutely presupposes the Old Testament. It is not a historical accident, but theologically fundamental that the "Bible" for Jesus and the New Testament authors is the Holy Scripture of Israel, and that the New Testament gospel is proclaimed in the language of these scriptures – more precisely and to a large extent in the language of the Septuagint. Only when the New Testament is read in connection with the Old Testament does Christian speech about God and His Christ, about the work of the Spirit, about creation, about the eschatological consummation, about the forgiveness of sins and justification, and about the proper way to lead one's life before God acquire its complete significance in the total context of God's action.

(58) *Second*, within the framework of the Christ event the Old Testament points to the New: not in the sense that it already openly attests the gospel of Christ when viewed under its historical literal sense, but in the sense that the *eschatological* self-revelation of the *one* God, who already communicates Himself as Himself in the Old Testament, occurs in the life, teaching, death and resurrection of Jesus Christ as articulated in the New Testament. For this reason Christians read the Holy Scripture of Israel as a document of their faith in a new way from the perspective of God's eschatological, salvific action through Jesus Christ.

(59) From this tension the theological unity of the two testaments is revealed in a *theocentric* perspective. The Old Testament attests God as He acts in history according to the perceptions of biblical witnesses in the foundational period of canonical revelation. He is attested as the living God, the one and only one who is present in Israel through His name, His Spirit and His truth, and who even in judging still proves Himself to be JHWH and the faithful God of the covenant. The New Testament attests God as the Father of Jesus who lets His kingdom come near through His Son (cf. Mk 1:14f.), gives His Son up to death (cf. Mk 9:31, 10:32–34, 14:41), raises him from the dead (cf. Mk 16:7; 1 Cor 15:4f.), exalts him at His right hand (cf. Mk 12:35f.; Rom 8:34; Heb 1:3f.; 1 Pet 3:22) and lets him return as the Son of Man at the Last Judgment (cf. Mk 8:38).

From the perspective of Christ the Old Testament is not merely a pre-history of Christian faith nor just a dialectical counterpart of the New Testament. Instead it is a record of the choice of Israel and Israel's history with God, in which Christianity is rooted (cf. Rom 11), and a document of hope for final salvation for Jews and Gentiles, a salvation which, due to God's fullness of grace, shatters the limits of space and time to realize the kingdom of God.

In the light of the Old Testament the Christ event is an eschatological completion of the gracious self-communication of God in history for the salvation of Israel and the nations, God's "Yes" to His promises (2 Cor 1:20), an unexpected realization of His salvific will which demolishes all borders.

When Christians read the *whole* Bible of the Old and the New Testament as the *one* and indivisible Holy Scripture, they embrace the religious inheritance of Israel, while at the same time seeing in the New Testament the document of God's eschatological action through Jesus Christ. This eschatological action gives to all who believe in him as the "Lord," the *one* Son of the *one* God (1 Cor 8:6), both Jews and Gentiles, hope for redemption through the justification of the godless and for the resurrection of the dead.

6 The Center of Holy Scripture and the Diversity of Its Theologies

(60) The unity of Scripture is not only problematical because of the difference between the two testaments, but also because of the great plurality of theological positions and conceptions collected in the scriptural texts. This diversity, which includes theological controversies and contradictions, is already prevalent within the respective testaments; it is even more visible when the entire Bible is taken into consideration. This makes it all the more important to describe the inner connection between the unity, totality and diversity of Scripture.

(61) The early church already recognized the *wealth* present *in the great variety* of biblical theologies.[58] In particular the newer forms of exegesis with their form-critical and redaction-critical studies have demonstrated the great extent of this variety while at the same time pointing out divergences, contradictions and confrontations among the different biblical positions. Admittedly, certainly not all the differences alleged in the history of historical-critical exegesis have been verified, nor are all the contradictions antithetical in nature. Yet all efforts to harmonize these different positions, like those undertaken in various circumstances throughout the history of biblical inter-

---

58 This topic is discussed in detail with regard to the tetrad of gospels in Irenaeus, *Adversus haereses*, III 11:8f. and Ambrosiaster, *Liber questionum veteris et novi testamenti*, suppl 3.

pretation, are not productive because they contradict the distinctive witness of each of the texts as well as their multifaceted influence throughout history.

(62) The diversity of Old Testament and New Testament theologies reflects the long period of time it took for Sacred Scripture to emerge as well as the great number of biblical authors, readers and transmitters with their varied and changing areas of experience. But this diversity also corresponds to the historicity of the revelatory action of God on the one hand and to the utterly all-embracing encouragement and demand of the biblical gospel on the other hand. In particular, however, the diversity of scriptural theologies mirrors the theocentrism of the gospel which gains in authenticity to the same degree that it is capable of reflecting God's essence and action in a large number of spectra, as it were, as that which is ever greater.

(63) While the polyphony of the biblical scriptures can be greatly appreciated in principle and in fact as an inner moment of the biblical gospel, it nonetheless pointedly raises once again the theological question concerning the unity of Holy Scripture as Old and New Testament.

The Church Fathers discovered the unity of Scripture, which they had to consider in their discussions concerning the extent of the canon, by way of allegorical, typological and analogical interpretations which were Christological in orientation. Lutheran, Reformed and Roman Catholic theologies of Scripture have taken up these methods of exegesis and worked forward from them, each in its own way with its own distinctive accents. It could be helpful for the formulation of an ecumenically binding understanding of Scripture if we examine these traditions, their theological-historical presuppositions, and their effects more closely and acknowledge their intentions.[59]

---

59 Details concerning this can be found in the relevant contributions in *Verbindliches Zeugnis I* (note 37) and in: W. Pannenberg and Th. Schneider, ed., *Verbindliches Zeugnis II: Schriftauslegung – Lehramt – Rezeption*, Freiburg, Göttingen 1995. The statement at the end of *Verbindliches Zeugnis I* [the "Joint Statement" which is printed in English as part of the present book] forms a basis for what follows.

6.1 The Evangelical-Lutheran Tradition

(64) The use of Martin Luther's formula "what promotes Christ" (from his preface to the Epistle of James in the September Testament of 1522[60]) as an orientation has proven to be extremely productive for Lutheran theology.

6.1.1 Martin Luther's "what promotes Christ" translates the *solus Christus* into the hermeneutics of Scripture (cf. *Werke. Kritische Gesamtausgabe* {"Weimarer Ausgabe"}, Weimar, 1883ff., 18, 606,24–31; 39/I, 47,41 and 49; ibid., *Deutsche Bibel* 7, 384,25f.). His postulate concerning the "clarity" (cf. ibid., 18, 609,5–14) and "self-interpretation" (cf. ibid., 7, 97,23f.) of Scripture refers to this Christocentrism. It does not necessarily result in a specifically Christological interpretation of Scripture, but introduces a material theological criterion into the interpretation of the Bible. On the one hand this Christocentrism emphasizes the alignment of the entire history of revelation attested in Holy Scripture with the Christ event; on the other hand it illuminates the certitude that not only New Testament writings, but also those of the Old Testament make statements about salvation which correspond to what the Christ event reveals eschatologically as the salvific action of God.

(65) The criterion was without doubt an appropriate means for grasping the Christocentrism of the New Testament gospel and, from this perspective, for arriving at significant differentiations among the different New Testament theologies. From a *Christian* perspective it was, however, also suited to recognizing the unity of *all of* Scripture. The objection is occasionally raised against this criterion that it is not capable of grasping the literal sense of Old Testament Scripture. Lutheran theologians do in fact recognize that it is not possible from today's vantage point to go along with many of Luther's individual exegeses here. But with good reason they can point to numerous statements of Luther which show that his formula, which has become no-

---

60 Prefaces to the Epistles of St. James and Jude, in M. Luther, *Werke* (note 43), *Deutsche Bibel* 7, 384–387. With respect to Luther's sharp criticism of the Letter of James expressed elsewhere, however, one should compare Melanchthon's *Loci* of 1559: "*Non igitur pugnat Iacobus cum Paulo*" (P. Melanchthon, *Werke in Auswahl*, R. Stupperich, ed., Gütersloh 1951ff., II, p. 126, 15f.).

thing short of proverbial, was not meant to narrow, but to open up the *entire* theology of Holy Scripture from the perspective of the Christ event. These statements also show that Luther quite clearly recognized and stressed the theocentrism of the Old Testament as well as that of the New Testament.[61] Guided by the New Testament (cf. Jn 1:1–18; 1 Pet; Heb) and following the Church Fathers, he was of course bound to the genuinely Christian conviction of faith that God has revealed Himself right from the beginning, in creation as well as in the history of Israel, and so also in the words of the Holy Scripture of the Old Testament, through His only-begotten Son Jesus Christ, and that consequently, from a soteriological point of view, a Christological hermeneutics makes precisely the theological tenor of the Old Testament evident. The texts of the Bible have many dimensions of meaning which also develop and change. Among these are the original and fundamental dimension of meaning at the time the texts were formulated and first made known; the expanded dimension which includes subsequent experiences that still occurred in the period when texts were being passed down within the Bible; the resultant dimension of meaning of Old Testament texts in the light of the Christ event; and the existing dimension of meaning *post Christum natum* which is contemporary at any given time.

6.1.2 (66) Already with Luther the "what promotes Christ" was combined in terms of its subject matter with a soteriology of *sola gratia* and *sola fide* that got its orientation not only from the Pauline *doctrine of justification*, but also from John and the First Letter of Peter. The theological dispute between Catholics and non-Catholics concerning this hermeneutics of Scripture was burdened for a long time with communication problems regarding the concept of faith. In the light of newer studies in the areas of exegesis and the history of dogma those traditional problems of communication can be regarded as overcome.[62]

---

61 All the prefaces to the Old Testament in the *Deutsche Bibel [German Bible]* are relevant.
62 Cf. K. Lehmann and W. Pannenberg, ed., *The Condemnations of the Reformation Era* (note 36), pp. 33–36, 49–56; *Lehrverurteilungen im Gespräch: Die ersten offiziellen Stellungnahmen aus den evangelischen Kirchen in Deutschland*, Göttingen 1993, p. 29f., p. 31f. (Conference in Arnoldshain), pp. 87–90 (United Evangelical-Lutheran

(67) Nevertheless, despite its high esteem for Pauline theology, the Roman Catholic tradition does not consider the apostle's doctrine of justification in the interpretation given by Luther as being the all-decisive standard for evaluating biblical theologies. Two things are important for ecumenical agreement: On the one hand, there must be increased willingness on the part of Protestants to differentiate between the doctrine of justification, that is the genuinely Pauline, and the doctrine as it is interpreted by Luther – without relativizing the significance of Luther's interpretation for ecumenism as a whole.[63] On the other hand, Roman Catholics must not only support a soteriology that makes it quite clear that justification only occurs through "one mediator between God and humankind, Jesus Christ (cf. 1 Tim 2:5)" and therefore only through "living faith (cf. Gal 5:6)"[64]; they must also recognize that the "doctrine of justification ... becomes the touchstone for testing at all times whether a particular interpretation of our relationship with God can claim the name of 'Christian'"[65]. If each side does its part there is no dissent on this point that would keep the churches apart, even if not all the differences between the Protestant and Catholic doctrines of justification have been eliminated.[66]

6.1.3 (68) The likewise typical dialectic of *law and gospel* as articulated by Luther in his adoption and reinterpretation of the distinction between "law" and "grace" found in Augustine (cf. *Werke. Kritische Gesamtausgabe* {"Weimarer Ausgabe"}, Weimar, 1883ff., 10/I, 2, 155,17–159,19 {Advent Pos-

---

Church of Germany), and p. 176f. (Faith and Order); "Gutachten des Päpstlichen Rates zur Förderung der Einheit der Christen" from Dec. 15, 1994, p. 34; *Stellungnahme der Deutschen Bischofskonferenz zur Studie "Lehrverurteilungen -- kirchentrennend?"* (The German Bishops, 52), Bonn 1994, p. 9f.

63 Cf. K. Lehmann and W. Pannenberg, ed., *The Condemnations of the Reformation Era* (note 36), p. 37.
64 Cf. *Stellungnahme der Deutschen Bischofskonferenz* (note 62), p. 9.
65 K. Lehmann and W. Pannenberg, ed., *The Condemnations of the Reformation Era* (note 36), p. 69.
66 Cf. ibid., p. 68.

til})[67] is closely connected to the explication of *solus Christus* found in the Lutheran interpretation of the Pauline doctrine of justification. This dialectic should not be used to distinguish between the Old and the New Testament; nor does it have as its goal the differentiation between gospel and ethics– as with the Antinomians.[68] It leads instead to a *total* view of Holy Scripture with regard to the effect Scripture has among its hearers through its proclamation. It is here that the unity of Scripture manifests itself in the great number of its voices inasmuch as, on the one hand, the proclaimed word of the Bible – as law – finds all hearers guilty of sin, placing them under the wrathful judgment of God (cf. ibid., 39/I, 434,3; 456,19–457,1), but, on the other hand and to a much greater extent, this same word – as gospel – in the preaching of the sermon, in absolution and in the sacrament makes the hearers certain through faith of the sin-forgiving grace of God (cf. ibid., 2, 467,12).

(69) This particular configuration of a Christocentric understanding of Scripture which was developed according to the theology of justification corresponds neither to the Reformed nor to the Roman Catholic tradition, and it has often been distorted in Lutheranism as well (see above). Moreover it suffers as a result of using neither "law" nor "gospel" in the biblical sense of those terms.[69] The following conviction, however, is in any case consistent with Reformed and Catholic teaching: In the process of the church's proclamation of the biblical message, the reality of God's love, which illuminates the abyss of human guilt in order to give the gift of true life, can be-

---

67 A similar distinction is that between "spirit" and "letter" which Luther makes, for example, in the First Lecture on the Psalms from 1513–1515 (in M. Luther, *Werke* {note 43}, 55/I, 4, 25f.).

68 Furthermore this dialectic does not include all the dimensions of his understanding of law, but articulates the "second", namely the "theological" use of the law (*usus theologicus, elenchticus*). The *primus usus legis*, the pedagogical and political meaning of the law, is to be differentiated from this. – To what degree the *tertius usus legis*, which was first advanced by Melanchthon, was approved by Luther, at least in terms of the subject matter if not verbatim, is under dispute. On this point cf. the contribution of U. Kühn in: W. Pannenberg and Th. Schneider, ed., *Verbindliches Zeugnis III. Schriftverständnis und Schriftgebrauch*, Freiburg, Göttingen 1998, pp. 161–180.

69 Cf. W. Pannenberg, *Systematische Theologie*, vol. III, Göttingen 1993, pp. 71–113.

come apparent through the power of the Spirit; and this soteriologically significant process corresponds to the basic structure of biblical speech about God.[70]

(70) At the same time, however, this means that the distinction between law and gospel cannot solve the problem of determining the relationship between the unity, totality and diversity of Scripture in its entirety, a problem which historical-critical exegesis in particular has exposed, since the sweep of God's action goes beyond the topic of sin / grace on which the controversial theological dispute focuses. Every attempt at a solution, however, will have to be judged by the extent to which it can incorporate what is intended by this distinction (also see 7 below).

6.2 The Reformed Tradition

(71) There is a close connection between Luther's "what promotes Christ" and Calvin's notion that Christ is "*unicus scopus totius scipturae*"[71].

6.2.1 It is not possible to explain Calvin's *Christocentric hermeneutics* as being a consequence of an allegorical interpretation of Scripture in the manner of the Church Fathers. His hermeneutics can be explained instead as a determination of the soteriological dynamic which, on the condition of Jesus Christ's pre-existence and mediating role in creation right from the beginning, reveals itself to Calvin in the biblical texts and also characterizes God's *one* covenant that spans both testaments (cf. *Institutes of the Christian Religion*, 1.7.1). More than anything else Calvin – much like Luther – gains a material argument from the recourse to Christ which should not only lead to the correct understanding of individual scriptural texts, but above all to the correct understanding of Scripture as a whole, the Old as well as the New Testament.

---

70 Canons 18–20 of the Council of Trent do not conflict with this either; cf. *Lehrverurteilungen – kirchentrennend? IV* (note 39), pp. 44–48.
71 A. Tholuck, ed., *Johannis Calvini in Novum Testamentum Commentarii curavit*, 8 volumes, Berlin, 1833–1865, VI (on 2 Cor 3:16).

(72) Consequently, the analysis of Calvin's hermeneutics of Scripture, when carried out under the influence of historical-critical biblical research, should be assessed in a similar way as in the case of Luther.[72] On the one hand the tensions between the postulated Christocentrism and the original historical meaning of Old Testament texts are obvious. On the other hand Calvin shows at least as clearly as Luther that the theory of Jesus Christ being *"genuinus sensus scripturae"*[73] does not result in the exclusion of certain texts of Holy Scripture but, on the contrary, justifies the insistence on its *entirety*. It also does not encourage a revival of allegorical exegesis, but is linked to a strict philological interest in the literal sense of the texts.

6.2.2 (73) Whereas Luther endeavors to understand the Christocentrism of the revelation event of the entire Bible as it is manifested in Holy Scripture by concentrating on the doctrines of justification and reconciliation discerned by Paul, Calvin places greater emphasis on the *revelatory quality of all of Scripture*, specifically naming the Old Testament as well. The unity of Scripture lies in the working of the Spirit who, as the same one who inspired the prophets, penetrates the hearts of the hearers in order to induce them to believe (cf. *Institutes of the Christian Religion*, 1.7.4). In a way that is comparable to the hermeneutical intention of the Lutheran dialectic of law and gospel, Calvin stresses the Spirit-caused *effect* of the scriptural message produced during preaching amongst the hearers who are ready to believe and in the church. By contrast, the modern question concerning the unity of Scripture begins above all with the subject matter and intentions of Scripture itself which are to be ascertained by exegetical means.

6.3 The Roman Catholic Tradition

(74) In Roman Catholic theology since the Council of Trent there has been intense reflection on the concept of revelation and on the authority of the

---

72 Cf. H. H. Eßer, "Die Lehre vom 'testimonium Spiritus Sancti internum' bei Calvin innerhalb seiner Lehre von der Heiligen Schrift,"in: *Verbindliches Zeugnis II* (note 59), pp. 246–258.
73 A. Tholuck, ed., *Commentarii* (note 71), III (on Jn 5:39).

church's teaching office with regard to the understanding and interpretation of Scripture (cf. DH 1507 [ND 215]). But there have been relatively few attempts to formulate a distinctive theology of Sacred Scripture which communicates its diversity and unity. Although the polyphony of biblical voices has been noted again and again and clearly addressed, until very recently, and with a clear anti-Reformational intent, this diversity was taken as proof of a certain obscurity of Sacred Scripture which could only become clear when judged by tradition and specifically by the church's magisterium. The statement that the authenticity of tradition and that of the magisterium are attributable to the working of the Spirit (cf. DH 1501 [ND 210]) was supposed to protect this position against the suspicion that a human authority was seeking to set itself up as judge of Sacred Scripture. This, of course, not only left unanswered the question concerning the Bible's power to criticize tradition and the church, which the Reformers focused on, but also and above all the question of how to understand the unity of Scripture itself in its relationship to the large number of texts and theological witnesses.

(75) The Second Vatican Council provided a *new approach* here even if it did not address the problem of "unity and diversity" directly.[74]

6.3.1 *Dei Verbum* begins with the concept of revelation which leads it to develop its theology of Sacred Scripture *in a theocentric perspective* (cf. *Dei Verbum* 2–6, 14–20). This theocentrism, however, is discussed in a soteriological and eschatological way. The Christ event thus forms the decisive point of reference: Already in the Old Testament God's plan of salvation is directed to the revelation of Christ (cf. *Dei Verbum* 15) while the New Testament texts not only attest this Christ event, but have also emerged in its course (cf. *Dei Verbum* 17).

---

74 Admittedly, many passages in *Dei Verbum* evidence the difficult struggle for consensus and compromise, also in the central areas of the understanding of Scripture and the determination of the relationship between Scripture and tradition. For background information see the commentaries of J. Ratzinger: *Lexikon für Theologie und Kirche*, 2nd edition, supplement 2, (1967), pp. 498–528, 571–581, and A. Grillmeyer, ibid., pp. 528–563.

(76) Under these circumstances the unity of Scripture is seen in light of the history of revelation: first of all in terms of its origin, with reference to the inspiration of the biblical authors or books (cf. *Dei Verbum* 11); secondly in terms of the biblical texts, with reference to the history of the self-communication of God which goes from the covenant with Abraham and Israel (cf. *Dei Verbum* 14 with reference to Gen 15:18 and Ex 24:8) to the "coming of Christ, the universal redeemer, and of the messianic kingdom" (*Dei Verbum* 15; cf. *Dei Verbum* 3–4); thirdly in terms of its content, with reference to that truth "which God wanted put into the sacred writings for the sake of our salvation" (*Dei Verbum* 11).

6.3.2 (77) The emphasis of *Dei Verbum*'s theology of Scripture is on the *"unity" of the books of Scripture* (*Dei Verbum* 11: "with all their parts"; *Dei Verbum* 12). In contrast, there are hardly any attempts in the document to differentiate among the various theological positions within Sacred Scripture. It is true that *Dei Verbum* 14 alludes to the patristic theme of divine instruction when it states that, "with God Himself speaking to them through the mouth of the prophets, Israel daily gained a deeper and clearer understanding of His ways and made them more widely known among the nations" (*Dei Verbum* 14, with reference to Ps 22:28f., 96:1–3; Isa 2:1–4; Jer 3:17). Furthermore the special significance of the four gospels is emphasized in the New Testament canon inasmuch as they are the "principal witness for the life and teaching of the incarnate Word, our Savior" (*Dei Verbum* 18). But this reflects little more than the Christocentric hermeneutics which, in its theocentric frame of reference, characterizes the entire theology of Scripture in the Constitution on Revelation. The problem exposed by historical-critical exegesis regarding the difference and (partial) contrariety of theological positions in the one Sacred Scripture is not addressed, although the document encourages biblical scholars to be differentiating in their text analysis and to interpret texts historically (cf. *Dei Verbum* 12).

6.3.3 (78) It is consistent with this theology of Scripture that the task of the church teaching ministry is still seen as the "authentic" interpretation of Scripture which is done "in the name of Jesus Christ" (*Dei Verbum* 10). The context makes it clear, however, that the exegetical work of investigating and differentiating texts cannot be restricted by this. Moreover, the point of the statement is certainly not to invoke a clear magisterial dictum as a way to remove the "obscurity" of Scripture, but, quite the contrary, to emphasize the *church magisterium's service to the word of God* as it is expressed in Sacred Scripture.

6.4 The Discussion Today

(79) As much as a current ecumenical understanding of Scripture has to include the different denominational traditions in order to arrive at an overall view that unites and leads forward, it also has to consider the contemporary context of the problems. This context is determined in terms of the texts by historical-critical exegesis and in terms of today's addressees by the distance between the biblical world of experience and the present time.

The denominational traditions converge in two essential points in the understanding of the center of Scripture: first in their return to God's salvific action which is assumed and testified in Scripture, and second in the Christocentrism of this revelation event.

(80) In the contemporary context the following differentiation must be made: On the one hand, the recourse to God's action both with regard to emphasizing theocentrism and with regard to insisting on the primacy of the *event* of revelation over the *witness* to revelation can easily be communicated to present-day biblical theology. On the other hand, we cannot ignore that tension exists between Christocentric hermeneutics and the original meaning of Old Testament texts as determined by historical-critical exegesis. But in the light of a theology that – in accordance with Christian faith – presupposes the unity of the Old and the New Testament Scripture, Christocentric hermeneutics is illuminating in that it bears witness to the revelatory action of God who communicates Himself as Himself eschatologically through Jesus Christ.

6.4.1 The Need to Make Distinctions in Keeping with the Gospel

(81) It is absolutely essential to prioritize and evaluate different theological positions. The problem arises when asking about the criteria for doing this. If we look at the history of historical-critical exegesis and biblical theology we recognize the great danger in applying standards of evaluation which seem plausible at one moment, but soon prove to be conditioned by their times and inadequate. But we also recognize the great opportunity to highlight the theological significance of Holy Scripture by means of prioritizations and differentiations.

Two principles must be borne in mind:

First: For their part, the hermeneutical criteria must be in keeping with Scripture; they only lead to a theologically appropriate understanding of the material if they are derived from the gospel which is articulated in the Old and the New Testament.

Second: Prioritizations and differentiations within the biblical scriptures must not call the unity of Holy Scripture into question, but lead to a better understanding of it.

6.4.2 The Discussions concerning a "Canon within the Canon" and a "Center of Scripture"

(82) The different attempts, especially in Protestant, but also in Catholic exegesis, to define a "canon within the canon" or a "center of Scripture" remain within the framework of theological controversies which do not touch the core of ecumenical theology. But due to fundamental hermeneutical considerations, they deserve our undivided attention all the same. We can see that these attempts, as different as they are in detail, endeavor to serve the purpose of giving the Old and the New Testament a clear theological profile without which one cannot discern the enduring obligatory nature of particular biblical statements. We must, however, also be alert to the danger of diminishing the importance of the indivisibility of Holy Scripture as well as to the

danger of underestimating the significance of those Old Testament and New Testament writings which, according to the respective conceptions, lie further from the "center" of Scripture or are even excluded from a "canon within the canon." The center of Holy Scripture can only be seen within the framework of its *unity* and *totality* – as these in turn can only be perceived from the center.

6.5 Unity through Diversity – Diversity through Unity: An Ecumenical Perspective

(83) The church must hear the witness to faith of *all* Old Testament and New Testament scriptures for the sake of its authentic proclamation of the gospel. But it also does not have to supplement the canon later: It finds *everything* it needs in terms of a normative foundation for its proclamation of the gospel in the scriptures of the Old and the New Testament.

6.5.1 The Entire Holy Scripture in Its Orientation towards God and towards Christ

(84) Catholics and Protestants can recognize themselves in the principle of their confession that the Holy Scripture of the *New Testament* has its theological unity in the orientation of all the different texts and traditions to Jesus Christ and through him to God. The manifold witnesses of the New Testament agree on the perception, retelling, profession, and reflection of God's eschatological, salvific action through the preexistence, incarnation, ministry, suffering, death, resurrection and glorification of His son *Jesus Christ*.

(85) With respect to the Holy Scriptures of the *Old Testament*, Christians of all denominations – together with the Jews – can recognize the theological unity of these texts in the many voices and long history of their orientation to God as the Lord of the whole world, of all time and of all life, who revealed Himself to Israel as the *one* God of its election. We Christians profess this God to be the one who, for the salvation of all believers, has revealed Himself eschatologically as the Father of Jesus.

(86) The following is true for both the Old and the New Testament: The differences present among biblical theologies open our eyes to the varied aspects of God's salvific action, not least of all with regard to its anthropological, ethical and ecclesiological dimensions. Conversely, precisely our strict orientation towards the theocentric salvation event gives us the freedom to make distinctions in terms of the significance of different theological statements and views within the Old and the New Testament. When we adhere to the unity and totality of Scripture we do not forgo the possibility of using Scripture itself to distinguish between the different theological positions of the biblical authors, nor does this require us to overlook possible biases and opinions conditioned by the times. And when we search for the "center" of Scripture we give ourselves the opportunity of discerning the unity and totality of Scripture in their inner tension.

6.5.2 The Unity and Diversity of Scripture – The Unity and Diversity of the Church

(87) The large number of theological positions assumed within the Old and the New Testament does not affirm the prevailing division among the churches. It represents instead a model of the church unity which corresponds to the Pauline image of *ecclesia* as the body of Christ (cf. 1 Cor 12:12–27; Rom 12:4f.): It is precisely because there is the *one* Spirit that there are the many gifts (cf. 1 Kor 12:1–11; Rom 12:5–6) and many members in the body of Christ; and when the *many* members accept each other as they are and perform their individual functions, the *ecclesia* realizes itself as the *one* body it always is in Christ. It is precisely because there are many voices in Old Testament and New Testament theology that the Bible forms a *unity* in its *totality* as a normative document of faith. And it is precisely because there is *one* God and *one kyrios* (cf. 1 Cor 8:6) that the large number of biblical witnesses to faith rings out in all its richness.

(88) Just as separate theological statements within the Old and the New Testament must not be isolated from the context of their situation, their theological intent, their theological theme and their location in *all* of Holy Scripture, so too must Christians accept that no one may be excluded from the church

for allowing *one* particular biblical (and specifically New Testament) theology influence him or her in a special way in the context of his or her faith in Christ. On the contrary, criteria of membership in the *one* church include holding on to the *whole* of Holy Scripture and recognizing the large number of theological, ethical, and spiritual impulses given by Scripture in different traditions within this one church.

7 Law and Gospel

7.1 Lutheran Theology

(89) In Lutheran theology the distinction between law and gospel has always played a decisive role as a criterion for the right interpretation of Scripture. According to Luther "almost all of Scripture and all theological knowledge ... depend on the correct understanding of law and gospel" (*Werke. Kritische Gesamtausgabe* {"Weimarer Ausgabe"}, Weimar, 1883ff., 7, 502,34f.; 1521; cf. 40 I, 207,17f.; 1531/35). With this distinction Luther and Lutheran theology are concerned with the proper definition of Holy Scripture's message about Christ as the gospel of the life-bringing mercy of God. "The gospel is good speech, news of peace about the Son of God who became flesh, suffered and rose through the Holy Spirit for our salvation" (*Werke. Kritische Gesamtausgabe* {"Weimarer Ausgabe"}, Weimar, 1883ff., 2, 467,12). According to Luther the gospel of Jesus Christ must be distinguished from the preaching and the reality of the law which is first and foremost useful for the recognition of sin.

(90) Because of the radical experience of sin in the life of a Christian the Lutheran Reformation resisted any attempt to let the law and its fulfillment become the condition for salvation and eternal life. Nonetheless, as shown in the first main section of Luther's Catechism, this does not rule out the possibility that for the Lutheran understanding of salvation good works in accordance with the commandments of God are the necessary result and the fruit of the gospel which has been received in faith, indeed that justifying faith itself is fulfillment of the first commandment.

(91) The different functions of the law are expressed in the theology of the Reformation by the doctrine of the threefold use of the law. Besides its function to find one guilty of sin ("*secundus et praecipuus usus*") the law has the function of a norm and a guide for action derived from faith ("*tertius usus*"). This normative use is the focus of attention in Calvin's works and is also found in the Formula of Concord. In addition to these there is the use of the law for maintaining external, temporal order ("*primus usus*").

(92) Newer Lutheran theology has moved beyond Luther's comprehension and frequently understood the law as a code word for the disastrous situation of humans on the whole from which they, who constantly stand accused, so to speak, are freed by the gospel of forgiveness and renewal. As a basic hermeneutical category for understanding Holy Scripture, this distinction then helps one maintain a clear view of the fundamental event of the "gospel" testified in various ways by the Holy Scripture of the Old and the New Testament as a liberating gift of the mercy and the life of God in Jesus Christ. The distinction also helps one avoid confusing or mixing up the gospel with "legal" threats or demands.

7.2 The "Catholic" Precursors

(93) The distinction between law and gospel found in the Lutheran Reformation has "Catholic", i.e. early church and medieval antecedents. Thus we encounter the distinction between law and word in Melito of Sardis, the theory of a gradually progressing divine revelation of the law in Justin and Tertullian, the distinction between law and grace in Augustine, and, based on this, the distinction between the old law and the new law as the law of the gospel and of grace in the Middle Ages. These distinctions referred primarily to the difference between the Old and the New Covenant and thus declared that the era of the law and the era of the word, of grace, and of the new law follow each other in salvation history. According to Augustine and Aquinas, the two eras differ chiefly in the following: The regulations of the law of God that were in force during the period of the Old Covenant could not in the end be fulfilled due to the weakness of human nature which permitted the law to become a letter of the law that destroys; on the other hand, during the period

of the New Covenant the strength and help needed to fulfill the will of God was given by the grace of the Holy Spirit. "*Lex data est, ut gratia quaereretur; gratia data est, ut lex impleretur*" (Augustine). Aquinas understood the new law in a very essential way as "law of the Spirit" (following Rom 8:2). But at the same time – above all in Augustine – the salvation-historical understanding that the two periods follow one another in sequence was also described in terms of the coexistence of the experience of failure because of the law of God and the experience of the re-creating grace of God in the life of Christians. As a result the dialectic which became the theme of the Lutheran doctrine of law and gospel was already envisioned.

(94) The Lutheran version goes beyond Augustine and the Middle Ages in three ways. First, that humans are condemned in their sin is not only considered to be a weakness of the law, but as God's very intention with the law; second, the righteousness of Christ bestowed in the gospel is a righteousness "outside of us"; and third, the motifs of consolation through the gospel and the certitude of salvation become the focus of attention. In Luther's early theology we also encounter the phrases "judgment and grace" or – following Augustine – "letter and spirit" in this context. In its dispute with the Reformation the Council of Trent later argued that the renewed life led according to God's law was the precondition for achieving eternal life.

7.3 The New Testament

(95) In the New Testament we do not encounter the formula "law and gospel" as such, but we certainly detect the antagonism between law and the grace which is efficacious through the gospel of Jesus Christ. In Paul the struggle for righteousness from works of law appears as a path which, through Christ (cf. Rom 10:4) or by faith (cf. Rom 3:28), has come to an end as a way to salvation. Here Paul is also visualizing a salvation-historical sequence that marks in particular the contrast between being a Christian and the piety of the Judaism of that era. This salvation-historical contrast is also discernible in the Gospel of John (cf. Jn 1:17). Paul characterizes the reality of the new covenant by referring to the "law of the Spirit of life in Christ

Jesus" (Rom 8:2). In the synoptic gospels the new reality is described as the dawning of the kingdom of God. Paul considers the law of the Old Testament to be a holy and good law of God which Christians can and must fulfill (cf. Rom 7:12; 13:8–10). This corresponds to the proclamation of Jesus in the synoptic gospels in which the law expresses the permanent "legal will of God" (W. Pannenberg; cf. esp. Mt 5:17–20). Nevertheless, according to Paul the life of a Christian is constantly being threatened by sin (cf. 1 Cor 10:12). At the same time all this shows that the structure of the interrelatedness between the covenant and the law of the covenant in the Old Testament is assimilated in the New Testament, although essential provisions of the Old Testament law – as, e.g. the legislation concerning sacrifice – are invalidated by the Christ event.

7.4 Hermeneutical Significance Today

(96) In light of this history and in consideration of its temporally conditioned form in the theology of the Lutheran Reformation the distinction between "law and gospel" has a *twofold* hermeneutical significance today for our understanding of the biblical message of the Old and the New Testament. *First,* it directs attention to the fact that in the witness of Holy Scripture we are dealing with the history of God's saving action and that Holy Scripture is authoritative for faith and proclamation today only when we take this salvation history into account which found its goal – and consequently also its criterion with regard to content – in Christ. *Second*, this distinction makes clear that the message of Holy Scripture concerns the gift of the mercy of God in ever new variations. With this gift God lets one share in His life in anticipation of the final consummation. With this gift the powers of sin, death and God's judgment which also threaten the lives of Christians are overcome and freedom is revealed as freedom for service and for community in love. This is a gift which on principle cannot ever be attained by human effort; it does, however, enable and compel humans to observe God's commandments with the binding obedience of faith.

(97) The hermeneutical criterion of law and gospel would, however, be *misunderstood* if it did not lead to the recognition that in the Old Testament

there is also the factual primacy of the "gospel", of the ever new bestowal of God's covenantal faithfulness and mercy, of the proofs of God's goodness and acts of deliverance, and of God's promises and prophecies.

The law as saving order of the covenant – though always at the same time as judgment on human disobedience – is intrinsically ordered to this understanding. The results of Old Testament exegesis, the concept of "gospel and law" in Karl Barth, but also the reflections of Gottlieb Söhngen which draw on Augustine and Aquinas have reinforced this insight. The "era of the law" is not a period without "gospel"; it is, however, aimed at the revelation of the fullness of grace in Jesus Christ.

(98) As a hermeneutical criterion law and gospel would also be misunderstood if one ignored the fact that the biblical gospel witnesses Christ as gift for the life in which reconciliation occurs not only as a non-imputation of guilt, but at the same time and above all as a new creation out of the Spirit for the praise of God's glory. The fruit of this new creation is love for the law as the good commandment of God as well as obedience to this law precisely in the social-ethical area of overall responsibility for the life of humans in this world. As a category of scriptural exegesis the duality of law and gospel does not exclude other distinctions – like, for instance, spirit and letter, judgment and grace, law and grace –, but when applied it heightens one's awareness in the manner presented here.

8 The Interpretation of Scripture in the Life of the Church

(99) The biblical texts emerged in the life of Israel, God's people, and in the church of Jesus Christ. They are oriented to making God known in worldwide dimensions and thus they are directed in a basic way to instructing in the faith and to building communities. In the process of the formation of the canon the church recognized the normativeness of the biblical writings while seeing itself, on the other hand, as "hearer of the word" who lives solely from that gospel testified in the Old and the New Testament scriptures. The significance of scriptural interpretation in the life of the church is grounded in this relationship.

8.1 The Interpretation of Scripture as a Fundamental Activity of the Church

(100) The church lives from Holy Scripture. Preaching, the sacraments, prayer and the love of neighbor are of elemental importance for the practice of faith and the understanding of the gospel. Reading and interpreting Scripture show Christians unmistakably and indispensably the underlying foundation and the guiding principle of their personal faith as well as the faith of the church. The questions about the quality, the intensity and the binding nature of scriptural interpretation are therefore essential questions about what being church means. The interpretation of Scripture is a fundamental action of the church. Possibilities for ecumenical agreement among the denominations grow to the same degree that the normativeness and sufficiency of Holy Scripture are not only asserted in the churches, but taken seriously theoretically as well as practically in theology, liturgy, service, and the confession of faith and are understood as making it possible to find a consensus in matters of faith in each new case.

(101) The forms of scriptural interpretation are as varied as the ways life is lived in the *ecclesia* itself. The liturgical use of Scripture is of special significance (see above, 3.1) since the "word of the living God" rings out in the midst of the celebrating congregation through the reading of the lessons, while the homily discloses the "gospel of Jesus Christ" to the congregation as the foundation and center of the liturgy as well as of witness and of service. The reading of Scripture has a similarly fundamental, albeit differently circumstanced status in the religious education of children, in religious instruction in school, in the catechesis of the congregation, and in the educational work of the church since fundamental knowledge about the Bible is not only imparted here, but the world of experience is also disclosed in a pedagogical way *sub specie Dei*. The scholarly interpretation of Scripture, however, which is indispensable for achieving certainty about the historical and theological origins of the *ecclesia*, is confronted with its own challenge. It works on perceiving the truth of biblical statements in their original form at the beginning of the development of biblical tradition by forming judgments which are well-founded and verifiable. At the same time it is concerned with discerning the factual coherence of these biblical statements and their rele-

vance in shedding light on experience. It then presents all these findings in dialogue with the other historical disciplines.

(102) All these forms of scriptural interpretation are indispensable for the church. To distinguish them precisely and then to connect them with one another from within is the hermeneutical prerequisite for bringing out the binding nature of Holy Scripture in the lived life of the church. The decisive *criterion* here is whether *the one* gospel of God's creative, judging and saving action which takes place definitively in Jesus Christ stands out in each interpretation.

8.2 The Interpretation of Scripture in the Liturgy

(103) In the Book of Nehemiah (7:73–8:18) the detailed description of the first Sukkoth celebrated in Jerusalem after the return from exile shows in an impressive way the central significance attached to the reading and the interpretation of Scripture in the worship of Israel. The "inaugural sermon" of Jesus in Nazareth developed in the Gospel of Luke (cf. Lk 4:16–21) continues the synagogal practice. The early Christian religious services take up this form. "When you come together, each one has a hymn, a lesson, a revelation" (1 Cor 14:26). In Colossians the Christians are encouraged as follows: "(W)ith gratitude in your hearts sing psalms, hymns and spiritual songs to God" (Col 3:16). In the pastoral letters the reading of Scripture is one of the most distinguished duties of the bishop (cf. 1 Tim 4:13; 2 Tim 3:14–17). Other passages indicate that New Testament texts were also soon being read within the framework of the gathering of the congregation. Paul ordered the congregation of Thessalonica to read his letter "to all of them" (1 Thess 5:27). Colossians 4:16 encourages the congregations to exchange the letters of Paul and to read them. In the Book of Revelation "the one who reads aloud the words of the prophecy" is blessed, "and blessed are those who hear and who keep what is written in it" (Rev 1:3).

8.2.1 The Use of Scripture in the Liturgy – Fundamental Considerations

(104) The celebration of the word of God in the words of Sacred Scripture opens up a multitude of possibilities to Christian liturgy for making use of Scripture. Dating back to the discernible beginnings of Christian worship there has been tension between the established forms and formulae of the word of God in the liturgy on the one hand and the word of God as it passes through the person of the preacher in the sermon on the other hand. This tension is connected to the fact that the sermon, unlike the basic liturgical acts of reading, praising, thanking, professing and petitioning, is supposed to provide the encouragement of the gospel for the lives of people today. The commission to preach is not yet completely fulfilled when Scripture is read without being interpreted. *Martyria* [witness] and *Liturgia* [worship] remain two basic forms of church life which refer to, but do not assimilate each other. That is why this tension should be maintained. In the history of the church one side or the other has often won out. The Reformation moved the sermon into the center of the religious service once again as the authentically apostolic way for the church to interpret Scripture. At the Second Vatican Council the Roman Catholic Church recognized quite clearly its deficiency in this respect and has tried to correct it: In all forms of worship with a scripture reading a sermon on the reading (homily) is at least recommended, and for Sunday and Holy Day Masses it is a binding prescription. For their part, Protestant Churches are once again discovering the richness of using and interpreting Scripture through the liturgy itself and are transferring this discovery into their agendas.

(105) In contrast to the theology of the East, the systematic theology of the Western denominations has only gradually begun to discover the importance of liturgical celebration and its connection to Scripture, an importance which has its foundations in the Old and the New Testament. Reflective theology's connection to Scripture has a *fundamentum in re* in the worship of the church in which the words are not only read, but made present in a celebratory manner, are meditated upon, and become the response of the people in their prayers. Christian worship lives from the revealed Word of God which, having been attested in the words of Sacred Scripture in a fundamental way, always makes itself relevant to the present. God's uninterrupted dialogue with hu-

mans which has a privileged, though not exclusive place in the worship of the church, is the condition for the possibility of speaking about God. At the same time worship, with its hopeful view of the consummation we are still awaiting, performs a critical function vis-à-vis theology by pointing out the limits of the same. With the determination of the canon of Sacred Scripture revelation came to an end in terms of "content", but not "formally": The mystery of our redemption must be proclaimed ever anew throughout the ages "until he comes" (1 Cor 11:26).

(106) The use of *scriptural texts* in the liturgy *puts them into a new context* which can open up new relationships for them with respect to their meaning. *On the one hand* this context is that *of all of* Holy Scripture which is to be understood as a unity from its Christological center and which the church's cycle of readings makes accessible in different ways and with different perspectives as a document of faith that establishes the church. *On the other hand* the context of liturgical Scripture reading is determined by *the ecclesia as a whole* and in particular by the office of preaching which is entrusted with the Scripture reading and the homily. Through the worship service the reading of Scripture is associated with the Credo in particular as the *regula fidei*, and in the celebration of the Lord's Supper with the memory of the suffering and death of Jesus as well as with the reception of the body and blood of Christ by the congregation. Above all the respective historical, social and cultural, and situational and personal contexts also have an effect on the reading and interpretation of Scripture in the religious service. Through readings and preaching the celebrating congregation is thus directed to the foundation and guiding principle of its religious existence; it is included in the community of those who live from the word of God which encompasses generations, nations, cultures and denominations; for its part it hears God's judging and forgiving, comforting and admonishing word "today" (Lk 4:21; Heb 3:7–19; 4:7) as it is proclaimed to it with the words of Holy Scripture.

(107) This generates a powerful hermeneutical field of tension. On the one hand, when Scripture is used in worship there can emerge considerable differences between its original meaning, which is to be reconstructed by means of exegesis, and its liturgical interpretation which makes Scripture relevant now. On the other hand, the praise of God takes place in the liturgy which is

what the biblical scriptures according to their fundamental meaning intend to express in the large number of texts and multiformity of genres.

(108) The use of Scripture in the liturgy is diverse and multiform. Christian worship consists of different liturgical celebrations each with its own form for using Scripture. The different text formats alone require our attention. The Greek liturgy is based on the Septuagint, the Latin liturgy on different translations, including but not limited to the Vulgate. Furthermore the liturgy sometimes takes liberties with the biblical text, especially in the hymns. Three levels should be differentiated: exact quotation, indirect allusion and motific reminiscence. The literary genres are frequently mixed. Thus the text of a hymn can have the character of a sermon, and a prayer can include elements of preaching. Regulative interventions like liturgical reforms have usually been responses to actual or supposed wrong turns the liturgy has taken. Sometimes these reforms have revealed the treasures of Sacred Scripture in a richer way, but at other times they have reduced the existing wealth through biblicistic regimentations. It is, however, quite correct to say that the Bible must always be a criterion for the authenticity of the church's liturgy. Nevertheless the specific hermeneutics of liturgical language and tradition must be taken into account.

8.2.2 The Scripture Reading

(109) The Scripture reading is the clearest instance of the literal use of Scripture in the liturgy. Guided by the synagogal worship service, while not dependent upon it, Christians produced cycles of readings early on which were organized according to different criteria. Common to all the churches, however, was that they read from the scriptures of the Old and the New Testament. The different groups of books were combined with each other in different ways. In this process the reading from the gospels was given the primary place in the liturgies of the East and the West.

(110) We should have a differentiated view of how the readings are understood with regard to the forms of celebration and the respective liturgical traditions. The spectrum extends from a catechetical recitation to a staged anamnestic proclamation. The liturgical presentation of the act of proclama-

tion differs accordingly as well as varying among the denominations. Both in the Roman Catholic liturgy and the Lutheran liturgy (similar to the Orthodox) the recitation of the gospel is understood as an act of *Christus praesens*.[75] In the liturgy of the Reformed churches, however, the epistle and the text of the sermon are in a context which is preordained by the theocentric and Christocentric theology of the *one covenant*.

(111) Notwithstanding the high esteem for Sacred Scripture in general we can observe that texts are dealt with rather freely in the liturgy. The biblical text is selected as a pericope or passage, occasionally arbitrarily; the beginnings are changed; abridged versions or omissions for other reasons alter the text; there are special forms like using tropes (inserted verses foreign to the text) and centones (combinations of various heterogeneous passages). These practices can increase the tension between the original context and the liturgical context of the scriptural passages to such a degree that the essential connection between the Bible and liturgy is obscured.

(112) Among other things the liturgical reform of the Reformation aimed at restoring the originality of the statements (cf. for example the German *Sanctus* from Martin Luther's German Mass). The liturgical reform of the Second Vatican Council was not only committed to the goal of providing the "table of God's Word" with a richer fare (*Sacrosanctum Concilium* 51), but also to the goal of making the importance of the scriptural reading for the religious service more apparent and to the goal of providing the liturgy as a whole with a greater proximity to Scripture.

(113) The use of Old Testament texts, which varies in the Christian denominations, is a separate problem. Often chosen only because of certain key-

---

[75] This can be illustrated by a number of ritual elements. In the present liturgy of the *Roman Catholic Church* these are the recitation of the gospel by the ordained officeholder, the posture of standing, the gospel procession with candles, the incensing, acclamations before and after the reading as well as the kissing of the book. In the liturgy of the *Lutheran Church* the acclamation of the congregation ("Glory to you, O Lord!"; "Praise to you, O Jesus Christ!") reflects the special status of the reading of the gospels.

words these texts lost their inherent meaning in the liturgies of the late period of antiquity and the Middle Ages and were increasingly eliminated from the cycles of readings. But reading from the Old Testament in worship opens up a great opportunity: The faith legacy of Israel is not only disclosed to the *ecclesia*, but the New Testament readings and sermon texts are also placed in the context of the entire biblical witness.

8.2.3 The Sermon as Interpretation of Scripture

(114) From time immemorial not only the reading of Scripture, but also the sermon has been part of the liturgy. Its crucial task is to make the words of support and the demands of the biblical gospel as expressed in the read words of Scripture accessible to the worshiping community. The sermon serves to make God's word real at the present moment and as such it is an essential part of the liturgy. It aims to help the hearers discern the current meaning of the gospel for the formation of their personal lives, and in so doing to strengthen the entire faith community.

(115) In the Roman Catholic understanding the homily is supposed to interpret the Scripture readings (but also other texts) of the liturgy. In the tradition of the Reformation the scriptural text for the sermon is chosen for the most part irrespective of the scriptural readings according to the cycle of pericopes, and it determines the theme of the sermon. In both cases the task is to bridge the gap between the liturgy with all its scriptural texts and everyday life. This requires on the one hand that the texts of Scripture be understood as inspired testimonies to fundamental experiences of faith and on the other hand that the "present time" (cf. Lk 12:54–57) be interpreted in a knowledgeable manner.

(116) Many people today have little appreciation of the liturgy and sermons. The conditions for communication in our contemporary society, which have undergone radical changes, are in great part responsible for this. If we take seriously the special way the revealed word is made present liturgically, we can also bring about a renewal of preaching in this challenging situation. The mystagogical preaching of the early church, which attempted to link the experience of the celebration with the everyday experience of the people, is

certainly a point of reference here. In addition the liturgy should of course also continue to put new forms of preaching into practice (e.g. dialogue sermons, "witnessing to faith" and many more) where those forms have proven successful. A basic prerequisite for a renewal of preaching is in any case an intimate knowledge of Scripture.

8.2.4 The Psalms in the Liturgy

(117) The Psalter has been of great importance for Christian liturgy since the first centuries. It conveys the faith experience of Israel to the worshiping *ecclesia* in the way this experience was consolidated in the psalms as thanksgiving, praise, lamentation, and petition. Both the understanding and the use of the Psalter in Christian liturgy are complex.

(118) Corresponding to the use of the psalms in the New Testament, the *Christological rereading* is also the primary, if not the exclusive motive for using psalms in the liturgy. Only rarely is the psalm used *ad litteram* in the liturgy. It is designated as unequivocally Christian by its position, its connection to other scriptural passages, and above all by its combination with specific antiphons as well as through the "*Gloria patri*" said at the end. This is particularly true of the Mass whose antiphons in the classical Roman liturgy are taken from the Psalter to a large extent. The Introit psalms of the Lutheran liturgies continue this tradition. The Reformed Churches take special credit for spreading the Psalter among the faithful through their composition of hymns from psalms and psalters of hymns. The existential relevance of the Psalter as it is made accessible in the liturgy acquires a new dimension for Christians inasmuch as they can regard Jesus Christ as *the* one praying the psalms or inasmuch as the psalm is directed to the glorified *Kyrios*.

(119) The Psalter has a special intrinsic value in the liturgy of the hours. In some instances there was and still is a continuity here with the use of the psalms in Judaism, especially with respect to the morning and evening psalms. The psalm is liturgically put to use in different ways. Originally it may still have been understood as a scriptural reading; the responsorial use, however, is also very old: A cantor sang the individual verses and the congregation answered with the responsory.

(120) As a responsory the psalm in the Eucharistic celebration of the Roman Catholic Church refers to the preceding reading from the Old Testament or the New Testament and is thus regarded less in its own right than as a "dialogue partner" of the Scripture readings. The Introit psalm of the Lutheran liturgy, however, provides the spiritual introduction to the worship service which is shaped by the additional readings from Scripture. For centuries the liturgy of the Reformed tradition has been marked by the use of rhyming psalms which, in their textual composition and musical setting, have incorporated the content and rhythm of the individual biblical psalms. This way of using psalms comes from the Geneva Reformation, and it has been renewed time and again since then. Along with other song material it determines the content of Reformed and other Protestant and Catholic hymnals all over the world to this day.

8.2.5 Other Old and New Testament Hymns of the Liturgy

(121) Like the psalms which have become hymns of the Christian liturgy, there are also other texts of the Old and the New Testament which have become meditations on the word of God through their recitation and musical form. To a significant degree they already received their linguistic form from the religious service of the synagogal or apostolic congregation and thus point to the close relationship between the Bible and the liturgy.

(122) In the classical antiphons of the Roman Mass, quotations from the gospel, for example, play a prominent role in the communion hymns. The idea of a double communion, expressed by the Second Vatican Council in the image of the two tables (cf. *Sacrosanctum Concilium* 51), has always assumed a convincing form here. The three New Testament canticles of the Lucan infancy narrative also have a very important place in the liturgies of the East and the West. As climaxes of the respective canonical hours they are proclamations in a twofold sense: both proclamations of salvation and praising responses. This is true in a similar way for many songs and hymns which have been handed down in the Pauline epistles and the Revelation of John. The beatitudes in the version of Matthew's Gospel are of special importance in the Byzantine liturgy where they are part of the Eucharistic celebration. The chant "Holy, holy, holy," which adopts a verse from Isaiah (6:3) and has

been expanded into a hymn through the Benedictus / Hosanna, stands in a prominent place at the center of the Eucharistic Prayer in the East as well as in the West.[76]

(123) On the one hand these references to the biblical hymns in Christian worship again indicate the freedom exercised by the liturgy in its use of the biblical heritage. This can be explained by the self-image of the church according to which the liturgy and the Bible arise in the end from *one* tradition. That also accounts for the smooth transitions between biblical passages and free verse which are obvious in some of the early Christian hymns that have been preserved. On the other hand by receiving, combining and interpreting these hymns in the liturgy the church makes use of the extensive possibilities of biblical speech about God.

8.2.6 Hymns and Songs Based on Biblical Quotations and Motifs

(124) Some of the poetic forms important for the liturgy are on the threshold between biblical and post-biblical elements of worship. A prominent example is the *Gloria* which should be dated back to the second century and was handed down among the *Odae aliae* of the *Codex Alexandrinus* (fifth century). The *Gloria* begins with a quote from Scripture (Lk 2:14). In the Eastern branch of tradition it utilizes a so-called psalm-*kathisma* (a compilation of verses from different psalms) as this is known in a similar form in the West through the parallel hymn *Te Deum*. Like the *Te Deum* the *Gloria* is a morning hymn.

(125) The liturgy was at first limited to biblical texts through the ban on the independent composition of hymns imposed in canon 59 of the Synod of Laodicea in 364. Soon, however, autonomous compositions once again enriched liturgical services. Especially Ephraem the Syrian (+ 373) in the East and Ambrose of Milan (+ 397) in the West helped the free composition of hymns gain new respect. The language used in these poetical compositions is by no means remote from the Bible. On the contrary, knowledge of Holy

---

76 This already involves a Christian transformation of Old Testament texts which, however, has its parallels in the synagogal tradition.

Scripture is the precondition for understanding the images employed. Liturgical poetry was first developed in the West within the framework of the liturgy of the hours. But during the course of the early Middle Ages it also found its way into the Eucharistic liturgy to an increasing degree through the addition of tropes (inserted texts) to liturgical texts and through the composition of sequences. In some cases these Latin texts were the starting points for the vernacular church hymns which had been emerging in a parallel manner since the Middle Ages. In the liturgy of the Reformation these vernacular hymns became central elements of the liturgical conversion of the biblical message. The Counter-Reformation hymns of the Roman Catholic Church picked up this thread, but they seldom achieved the theological quality of the hymn tradition in Protestantism. Hymns of Protestant provenance were soon included in Catholic hymnals, usually in an adapted form and anonymously.

(126) To this day *church hymns* are an important factor for communicating the biblical message to a particular age. Biblical motifs and images are often used in the so-called "new spiritual songs." But here as with traditional liturgical texts we are faced with the problem that the distance between young people and the language of the Bible is growing so that many of the thematic allusions are no longer understood.

8.2.7 Liturgical Prayer

(127) The Bible has also left its mark on liturgical prayer in various ways. Many Old Testament and New Testament passages and formulae are used verbatim as prayers in the Christian liturgy. This is true of the psalms, for instance, which appear in their entirety or as separate verses (e.g. in the opening calls to prayer found in the hours of the day) in the liturgies of the East and the West. *The* biblical prayer *per se*, however, is the Lord's Prayer. We can recognize its significance especially in the fact that it, like almost no other biblical text, forms the bridge between personal and liturgical spirituality.[77]

---

[77] The motives for including the Our Father in the Eucharistic liturgies of the East and of the West, which has been the case since the fourth century, are different. The Ro-

(128) A special case of the liturgical use of scriptural passages is the "Eucharistic embolism" or account of institution in the Eucharistic Prayer. Up to the time of the Reformation none of the known early Christian liturgies had adopted one of the biblical accounts of the institution of the Eucharist word for word. Instead this was an independent strand of tradition which was of course subjected to constant correlation with the biblical tradition until it was definitively fixed in the major Eucharistic liturgies.

(129) Whereas the Eastern liturgy makes abundant use of scriptural quotations in the texts of its prayers, the Roman tradition is more restrained here. But it, too, lives from the spirit of the Bible. Many collects of the Roman sacramentary tradition acquire an unexpected depth when the biblical context, which is often only implied in indirect allusions and individual concepts, is revealed. Yet it cannot be denied that the anamnestic element plays a rather subordinate role with respect to the scriptural references in the prayers of the Roman tradition.

(130) Acclamations and formulae are special elements in the realm of liturgical prayers since they stand in an often uninterrupted continuity with the biblical tradition to this day. Salutations, formulae of approval and homage, as well as doxologies guarantee, in some cases right down to the language itself, that the biblical heritage is present in the Christian liturgy. It is remarkable that precisely those parts of the liturgy which have been assigned to the congregation have survived in Hebrew, Aramaic or Greek, like the *Amen*, the *Hallelujah*, the *Hosanna* or the *Kyrie eleison*. Such formulae serve to ensure that we stand in a common, unbroken tradition. Knowledge of the exact meaning of the words is less important here than the act of approval or praise. This makes it clear that the liturgy does not convey the biblical message exclusively through words. The message takes shape instead within a complex framework of verbal and nonverbal communication.

(131) Nonverbal expressions, symbols, gestures, and ritual actions, which should of course always be interpreted in the context of the words of Scrip-

---

man liturgy refers to its "divine institution" (cf. Mt 6:9) which underlines the dignity of the text as the "Lord's Prayer."

ture, join the forms cited here in which Scripture has been received into the liturgy. The connection of these different dimensions occurs primarily at the level of experience, but at the same time it also needs to be developed mystagogically. Here, too, the danger is particularly great at the present time that these elements will be misunderstood, but we are also presented with the marvelous opportunity to intensify the active participation of the faithful in the liturgy.

8.2.8 The Diversity of Scriptural References and the Unity of the Liturgical Witness to Faith

(132) The diversity of the use of Scripture in the liturgy, which is seen above all in historical perspective and in ecumenical comparisons, reflects the diversity inherent in Sacred Scripture itself, which is an exact expression of its totality and unity and its spiritual and theological richness. On the other hand, even with all the denominational differences that exist in the field of tension between the Bible and liturgy, the use of the Old and the New Testament for liturgical *lectio* and preaching, which is common to all denominations, in conjunction with any other recourse to Scripture in the worship service bears witness to the unity of the church which is grounded in the will of its *Kyrios*.

8.3 The Scholarly Interpretation of Scripture in Exegesis and Systematic Theology

(133) The rich forms of liturgical, homiletical and catechetical reading and interpretation of the Bible as well as private meditation on Scripture are fundamental to the church. But they in turn also depend on scholarly analysis and interpretation of the Bible. Otherwise it would not be possible when understanding and using Scripture "to make your defense to anyone who demands from you an accounting for the hope that is in you" (1 Pet 3:15). That is why a form of scholarly interpretation has also always been part of the ecclesiastical interpretation of Scripture from very early on. It is in fact indispensable for the church so that the faithful can recognize what is contained in the binding witness of Sacred Scripture.

(134) The tasks, concepts and locations of scholarly exegesis have changed considerably over the course of time. The modern situation is marked in particular by the emergence of historical-critical methods in exegesis. The reconstruction of the "literal meaning" by means of philological and historical methods is actually the foundation of *every* interpretation of Scripture, but in particular of its scholarly interpretation. Nevertheless important distinctions still have to be made: The task of interpreting Scripture has not only been given to exegesis, but also to systematic theology.[78]

(135) *Exegesis* covers the range of the "literal sense" of scriptural testimony. This means that it studies the changes in the sense of Scripture by means of literary criticism, the history of religion, form criticism, redaction criticism, and tradition and reception criticism. Consequently it uncovers the historical form which the "truth of the gospel" (Gal 2:5,14) had originally assumed through the revelatory action of God and eschatologically through the Son of God, the Word of God which "became flesh" (Jn 1:14).

(136) The *systematic interpretation of Scripture* presupposes the "historical-critical" reconstruction of the "literal sense." Its tasks are to present "the mystery of the faith" (1 Tim 3:9), which is witnessed in a literary and historical way in the biblical texts, in its ongoing and current significance for the church and theology, and to confirm it in a reflective, deliberative way in the dialogue with the other scholarly disciplines.

(137) *Cooperation* between the exegetical and the systematic-theological interpretations of Scripture is especially necessary in contemporary theology. Exegesis can be saved from hermeneutical blindness and systematic theology from a historical vacuum. Conversely, exegesis becomes more aware of the claim to truth of the biblical texts and systematic theology of the biblical foundation of all religious knowledge. It is precisely the dialogue between exegesis and systematic theology on Sacred Scripture that will strengthen the inner connection between scholarly and ecclesiastical, especially homiletical, interpretations of Scripture, in particular by making possible a new kind of spiritual reading of Scripture.

---

78 Cf. Vatican Council II, "Decree on the Training of Priests" (*Optatam totius*) 16.

8.4 The Significance of the Interpretation of Scripture for Ecumenism

(138) The reception of historical-critical methods of exegesis took very different courses in the churches. As a result considerable denominational tensions built up at first. In the meantime newer developments in the understanding of the science of exegesis and in its interpretive practice as well as in the churches' understanding of theology have made the scholarly interpretation of Scripture into a productive component of ecumenical theology.

8.4.1 The Development in Protestant Theology and in the Protestant Church

(139) The historical-critical exegesis of the Old and the New Testament arose and was cultivated above all in the realm of Protestant theology. The question concerning the *sensus literalis et historicus*, which, even if assessed differently, had been posed over and over again since the time of the early church, was one impulse. Another was humanism which had at first also been able to provide Catholic exegesis with important stimuli (through Erasmus of Rotterdam or Richard Simon). The scriptural principle of the Reformation which had been linked to a new understanding of the historical interpretation of Scripture in the eighteenth century (Semler) was crucial. But in the end it was also the Enlightenment with its radical criticism of the Bible and the church that influenced historical-critical exegesis (Reimarus) such that the long-term effects occasionally cause mistrust to this day.

(140) During the course of the nineteenth century three essential tasks of "historical-critical" exegesis took shape in connection with the development of historical thinking: (1) the investigation of the history interpreted in the biblical texts; (2) the philological analysis of the biblical texts; and (3) the explanation of their historical sense as intended by the author or redactor. All three tasks were to be accomplished by means of methods which did not have a specifically theological character, but were universally accepted as scholarly. Especially the methods employed in historical and literary studies, and later those used in sociology, linguistics and comparative religion were considered suitable.

The use of these methods and principles secured a permanent place for biblical exegesis in the university since the utilization of historical-critical research procedures corresponded to a large extent to the educated class's awareness of problems in the period following the Enlightenment. Moreover, an alliance between historical-critical exegesis and liberal theology was emerging which, with its claim to carrying out research in an unprejudiced manner, seemed to provide a logical response to the challenge of the Enlightenment.

(141) There was of course recurring and persistent opposition to the results of historical-critical biblical research and to its hermeneutics. This occurred because exegesis challenged many traditional views about the history of the origin of the Bible, did not take the inspiration of Holy Scripture into consideration methodologically, and often clashed with Protestant "orthodox" and pietistic beliefs in its explanation and theological assessment of scriptural texts. This opposition was also evidenced in the discussions of academic theology. Nonetheless, historical-critical exegesis had a strong influence on large segments of Protestant theology and the Protestant Church, not least of all because of its recognized status at university-level educational institutions: It understood how to fill the *sola scriptura* with life in a new way; it opened up new perspectives to biblical preaching; and in all of Protestant theology it made it possible to turn to the Bible as a historically understood text.

(142) In retrospect, however, we see not only the strengths, but also the limitations and deficits of historical-critical exegesis. These do not result from the fact that historical and literary methods were applied in the interpretation of Scripture, but from the fact that, for a long time, exegesis could extricate itself only with difficulty from rationalistic and positivistic tendencies which other theological disciplines had of course also embraced. As a result the theologically important questions concerning inspiration, canonicity and the unity of Holy Scripture faded far into the background or were dismissed out of hand as in principle unscholarly.

(143) It is all the more important to note that opposite trends can also be observed in the more recent history of Protestant exegesis. Karl Barth's de-

mand that one should carry out a *theological* interpretation of Scripture, taking the word of God as the starting point,[79] has, however, only been partially adopted in exegesis, especially since it poses hermeneutical problems of its own. Existential theology[80] has used Heidegger's hermeneutics in its own way for the benefit of exegesis. One can explain redaction-critical exegesis not least of all from its theological interest in what the biblical authors intended with their message. Canonical exegesis (the "canonical approach")[81] tries to implement the premises of dialectical theology directly, whereas a reception-aesthetic approach in exegesis seeks to fulfill Hans-Georg Gadamer's demand to develop an awareness of the problems which takes into account the effective history of a text.[82] In the newer conceptions of Protestant scriptural hermeneutics[83] scholars not only criticize the positivistic temptation of conventional historical-critical exegesis[84], but also place stronger emphasis on the church's responsibility for the scholarly interpretation of Scripture[85].

---

79 Cf. K. Barth, *Kirchliche Dogmatik*, vol. 1: "Die Lehre vom Wort Gottes," part 2, Zurich: 1948, pp. 505–598 (§19).
80 Cf. R. Bultmann, *Glauben und Verstehen*, vol. I–IV, Tübingen: 1952–1965.
81 Cf. B. S.Childs, *Biblical Theology of the Old and New Testaments: Theological Reflection on the Christian Bible*, London: 1992.
82 Cf. H.-G. Gadamer, *Wahrheit und Methode: Grundzüge einer philosophischen Hermeneutik*,Tübingen: 1960, 6th edition 1990.
83 The following book gives a survey of different pastoral and academic methods of interpretation and application: *Das Buch Gottes: Elf Zugänge zur Bibel. Ein Votum des Theologischen Ausschusses der Arnoldshainer Konferenz*, Neukirchen-Vluyn: 1992.
84 Cf. W. Pannenberg, "Heilsgeschehen und Geschichte," in idem, *Grundfragen systematischer Theologie (I): Gesammelte Aufsätze*, Göttingen: 3rd edition 1979, pp. 22-78.
85 Cf. P. Stuhlmacher, *Vom Verstehen des Neuen Testaments: Eine Hermeneutik*, Göttingen: 1979, 2nd edition 1986.

8.4.2 The Development in Roman Catholic Theology and in the Roman Catholic Church

(144) The Roman Catholic Church had a very reserved view of historical-critical exegesis for a long time. The "Oath against the Errors of Modernism" (cf. DH 3535–3550 [cf. ND 143–143/13]) and most of the decisions of the Pontifical Biblical Commission[86] up to the middle of the twentieth century not only showed extreme skepticism toward exegesis that worked with historical-critical methods, but also resulted in a massive obstruction of the independent and responsible work of Catholic theologians. It was not until mid-century that the Bible movement and the ecumenical movement initiated a change. Pius XII's encyclical *Divino afflante Spiritu* of September 30, 1943 (cf. DH 3825–3831 [cf. ND 232–236]) marked an important stage in this development.

(145) Of even greater importance was *Dei Verbum*, the Dogmatic Constitution on Divine Revelation of the Second Vatican Council.[87] In the context of a new reflection on the normativeness of Sacred Scripture the teaching office not only revealed its complete willingness to accept the historical and literary methods of exegesis, but also to promote them. The text recommends quite emphatically the exact, scientific investigation of the environment of the biblical scriptures, the conditions surrounding their origins, their forms and genres, and the intentions behind their statements. In the context of an understanding of inspiration that focuses on the communication of the "truth" necessary for salvation (cf. *Dei Verbum* 11) the document likewise assigns exegetes the task of paying attention "to the content and unity of the whole of Scripture" (cf. *Dei Verbum* 12). Initially literary-critical, form-critical and redaction-critical methods achieved broad acceptance in Catholic exegesis in the period following the Council; the question concerning the unity of

---

86   Cf. *Enchiridion Biblicum*, Naples, Rome: 4th edition 1961; *Enchiridion Biblicum: Documenti della Chiesa sulla Sacra Scrittura*, Latin – Italian, Bologna: 1993.
87   The Pontifical Biblical Commission's "Instruction on the Historical Truth of the Gospels" (*Sancta mater ecclesia)* from April 21, 1964 (DH 4402–4407 [cf. ND 240–245]) prepared the way for this document.

Scripture has only recently received increased attention in Catholic biblical studies.

(146) The Pontifical Biblical Commission's document "The Interpretation of the Bible in the Church" published in 1993[88] displays great openness in its recognition of different approaches to the Bible. It not only supports the use of the proven methods of historical criticism, but also the utilization of newer instruments of analysis in the scholarly interpretation of Scripture. The "fundamentalist" use of Scripture is sharply criticized insofar as it rejects critical biblical research *from the start* and does not take the historical character of biblical writings into account. The document does not highlight a particular methodology as the mark of Catholic exegesis, but the consistent use of all the research methods which serve the historical investigation of Scripture. Over and above that, it emphasizes the dynamic involvement with the ecclesial effective history or living tradition of Sacred Scripture which emanates from the Bible itself.

(147) In fundamental agreement with the magisterium, the newer forms of Roman Catholic theology stress the freedom of exegetical research and teaching in the sense that their analysis and interpretation of biblical texts are bound by scientific criteria. At the same time they stress the ecclesial responsibility of exegesis which is not demonstrated by curtailing scientific precision, but by developing a hermeneutics that is in keeping with the texts themselves and with their original effective history or living tradition.

8.4.3 The Ecumenical Significance of the Scholarly Interpretation of Scripture

(148) Exegesis of the Old and the New Testament has become a theological discipline which is capable of providing ecumenism with important stimuli. Shared prerequisites have been the use of historical and philological methods and the obligation to explain and understand Scripture historically. The close, collegial exchange of ideas as well as the development of joint exegetical and

---

[88] Pontifical Biblical Commission, "The Interpretation of the Bible in the Church" (April 23, 1993), in: *Origins*, January 6, 1994.

biblical-pastoral projects have been helpful. Up to the middle of the twentieth century it might have seemed as if there were an indissoluble unity between the *sola scriptura* as understood by *Protestants* and historical-critical exegesis to the extent that its work on the original historical sense of Scripture made the *extra nos* of the salvation event clear. For several decades now a different picture has been emerging through the work of exegetes which is connecting them ecumenically. On the one hand, Catholic theology has become more aware of the significance which Holy Scripture possesses as the source and norm of faith; on the other hand, the insight has evolved in both Protestant and Catholic theology that the coexistence of Scripture and tradition which can be observed in the development of the Bible itself is capable of stimulating ecumenical thinking.

(149) Ecumenical cooperation itself thus promotes exegetical research since the dialogue between the denominations with their respective traditions of understanding and interpreting Scripture can sharpen biblical scholars' awareness of the problems. Conversely, every exegesis of a text results in an encounter with Holy Scripture which not only gives rise to the demand that there be *one* church, but, with the original witness to Christian faith, also lays the only sound foundation for a church unity which is in keeping with the gospel.

8.5 The Significance of Scholarly Exegesis for the Church's Interpretation of Scripture

(150) In an elemental way the community of believers needs to hear the word of God in the words of Sacred Scripture so that this becomes the source and guiding principle of its faith. That can only occur if the church is aware of the binding nature of Scripture in each of its periods and in its historical situation. The church has the possibility of perceiving the gospel as "the power of God for salvation to everyone who has faith" (Rom 1:16) and of having it be efficacious by virtue of the Spirit. In its liturgical, homiletical and catechetical use of Scripture the church is exposed to the danger that it only detects the echo of its own convictions of the past and the present in the Bible of the Old and the New Testament. In principle no generation or de-

nomination is immune to the danger of monopolizing Scripture. Theology is exposed to this danger as well. Nonetheless, theology can also contribute to minimizing the danger. Exegesis in particular is able to do its part for the gospel, especially by using methods and adhering to hermeneutical principles in its analysis and interpretation of Sacred Scripture which, within the framework of what is available to scientific reasoning, promise to increase knowledge about the sense of Scripture that is normative for the church. On the one hand, exegesis, understood as the theological interpretation of Scripture, presupposes the *sensus fidelium* which consists primarily in the knowledge and acknowledgment of the word of God in the words of Sacred Scripture. On the other hand, the knowledge of faith and the life of faith of the *ecclesia* depend in an indispensable way on the insights and stimulation of the scholarly interpretation of Scripture with respect to its inquiries into the original sense of the Bible. The church acquires certitude about its historical foundations in this original sense of the Bible.

8.5.1 The Doctrine of the Multiple Senses of Scripture

(151) The doctrine of the multiple senses of Scripture as it was reflected upon and applied in many variations throughout the centuries was developed by patristic and medieval theologians as a response to questions concerning the theological content of Scripture and the ecclesial significance of scriptural interpretation.[89] Under the conditions of "pre-critical" exegesis it connected the knowledge that the "spirit" should be disclosed through the "letter" of Scripture with the search for an actualization of the texts. This actualization was supposed to disclose those dogmatic, ethical and eschatological senses of Scripture that lie beyond the immediate situation in which the biblical texts emerged and that illuminate their theological meaning for each contemporary period of the church.

(152) The view was already widespread in early Jewish and early Christian times that Old Testament scriptural texts have an allegorical meaning. With

---

89 Cf. H. Graf Reventlow, *Epochen der Bibelauslegung*, vol. I: *Vom Alten Testament bis Origenes*, Munich 1990; vol. II: *Von der Spätantike bis zum Ausgang des Mittelalters*, Munich 1994; vol. III: *Renaissance, Reformation, Humanismus*, Munich 1997.

the Church Fathers the allegorization also included the New Testament, especially the gospels and the Apocalypse of John.[90] The conviction that a higher, spiritual sense was written into the literal sense corresponded to the classical perception of truth; it resulted in an interpretation of Scripture which was comparable in its method to the exegesis of Homer. It did not, however, open itself to the syncretism of classical antiquity, but sought to appreciate the unity of the two testaments and the connection between Scripture and church tradition.

(153) Alexandrian exegesis forced the distinction between the "literal" and the "spiritual" senses of Scripture to such a degree that the spiritual was considered to be the true sense of Scripture, which, however, could not be disclosed without the literal sense of *all* of Sacred Scripture. In contrast the Antiochians placed greater emphasis on the fundamental meaning of the literal sense of even individual texts. Unlike some of the Alexandrians they saw this sense not only in the historical content of the information, but also in the historical intention of the author.

(154) In the theory of the four senses of Scripture developed later in the West, three spiritual senses were classed with the literal sense: the "allegorical" with which the "dogmatic" meaning was detected, the "moral" with which ethical-spiritual consequences were drawn, and the "anagogical" with which the eschatological meaning of the text was illuminated. The frames of reference for the allegorization were, on the one hand, *all* of Sacred Scripture, which was read from the perspective of a Christocentric soteriology, and, on the other hand, the church's understanding of faith arising from tradition in each respective period, which was seen to be in essential agreement with the theology of the Bible. Irrespective of the use of the four senses of Scripture, in particular in the spiritual interpretation of the Bible, the medieval theology of the West (above all Thomas Aquinas[91]), in the wake of

---

90 Origen mentioned the essential elements of this hermeneutics in the preface to his *Peri Archon* ["On First Principles"].
91 Proofs for this can be found in O. H. Pesch, "Exegese des Alten Testaments bei Thomas," in: *Deutsche Thomas-Ausgabe*, vol. 13 (1977), pp. 682–716.

Augustine, advocated a priority of the literal sense for determining the doctrinal content of Scripture.

(155) Otherwise the use of the method of the fourfold sense of Scripture had already become problematical since the twelfth century (the Victorines) as a result of arbitrariness and misuse. The Reformation deepened this crisis by criticizing not only certain allegorical interpretations, but the concept as such. The Reformers discussed the problems of the unity of Scripture and tradition, which for the most part was presupposed in allegorical exegesis, and they understood the Christological center and unity of Scripture specifically in the light of justification as witnessed by the Apostle Paul. Both Luther and Calvin still used the allegorical interpretation of Scripture in their sermons, but they focused on the literal sense, in part programmatically, in both their exegetical and dogmatic argumentation. Over and above that the church's understanding of faith and Scripture was frequently challenged in principle during the course of the Enlightenment; in many instances rational biblical criticism radically doubted the historical informational content as well as the theological integrity of Scripture. In Catholic theology the allegorical or typological interpretation, in particular of the Old Testament, endured for quite a while. But to the same degree that Catholic exegesis was receptive to historical-critical methods the doctrine of the fourfold sense of Scripture receded in Catholic theology as well.

(156) In our attempt to appreciate this doctrine from a contemporary perspective, we must make some distinctions. *On the one hand* we cannot overlook the weaknesses of this hermeneutics. It favored a harmonization of the different theological ideas within the Old and the New Testament. In general it resulted in a rather considerable relativizing of the original meaning of scriptural texts. Because of its approach this hermeneutics had difficulty distinguishing between the historical sense of Scripture and the prevailing perception of faith. It could not be readily combined with the modern sensitivity for the history of biblical revelation. But above all this hermeneutical approach lacked a programmatic mediation and a fundamental clarification of the relationships between the literal and allegorical senses of Scripture. In the controversy surrounding the interpretations it was not at all uncommon for one to be faced with the problem of deciding which allegorical

interpretation (among many) should have a claim to validity. In this context influential theologians stressed time and again the fundamental importance of the literal sense or the facts expressed in the literal sense for the allegorization; in disputes about the truth of faith only the literal sense counted anyway. Nevertheless, it must be admitted that in exegetical theory and practice questions concerning the significance of the literal sense of Scripture for the spiritual sense remained unanswered to a large extent. But after the breakup of church unity in the Latin West and the advance of the Enlightenment's fundamental criticism of biblical revelation it became imperative to ask these questions in a new and radical way and to answer them. The fourfold sense of Scripture, however, was not capable of accomplishing this.

(157) *On the other hand* the matters expressed in the doctrine of the fourfold sense of Scripture are still important. By way of allegorization theologians were successful in applying biblical texts extensively. There is no doubt that this doctrine produced a wealth of scriptural theologies and scriptural spiritualities which are capable of enriching theology, preaching, piety and the practice of faith to this very day. The doctrine also opens our eyes at the present moment to the fact that the texts of Scripture have spiritual, ethical and kerygmatic dimensions which are not apparent in the original meaning of these texts as verifiable with historical-critical methods, but that are nonetheless part of their genuine potential for meaning. It remains an important task to ascertain how we can take up this issue within the horizon of contemporary thinking.

8.5.2 The Search of Exegesis for the Historical Sense of Scripture and the Question concerning the Binding Nature of Scripture

(158) At present the scholarly interpretation of Scripture is marked by the reception of historical-critical methods in exegesis. But there is also a scholarly interpretation of Scripture – on the basis of exegetical work – in systematic theology. We can only recognize the significance of exegesis for the church if we also consider its relationship to systematic theology.

8.5.2.1 The Hermeneutical Approach of Exegesis

(159) Corresponding to the contemporary awareness of problems, exegesis has the obligation, in accordance with its ecclesial mission, to explain the meaning of every single biblical text at every stage of its historical genesis and to understand it in the context of the entire Bible – as far as this is possible and without contriving false alternatives between the *author's intention, the reader's reception and the text's meaning*. In addition, exegesis is to investigate the assumptions, objectives and consequences of the inner-biblical processes of reception, determine the structure, content and pragmatics of the different theological concepts of the biblical theologies, and draw historical and theological comparisons between them. Moreover, if exegetes take to heart that the texts are to be understood on the whole as testimonies to God's action towards His people and in the entire cosmos, then these exegetes will also be led to the genuinely *theological* question concerning that which has been attested in the biblical writings, concerning its reality and truth. This ultimately leads to the questions concerning the center, the totality and the unity of Scripture. (See above, 4.1–2; 6,4–5.)

(160) The historical question remains the leading issue in all this since the Bible received its phrasing and its form in a period long past. Exegesis uses primarily historical and philological methods; it asks in a fundamental way about the original meaning of the scriptural texts and thus protects against the danger of reading contemporary concerns into the text. Exegetes familiarize themselves with the traditions of ecclesial and general cultural understandings of Scripture in order to sharpen their awareness of the problems, but they also create the prerequisite for a rationally justified distinction between the original meaning of Old and New Testament texts and the meaning perceived in the history of their interpretation.

(161) The original meaning of biblical writings, as contemporary exegesis seeks to investigate it, is not necessarily identical with the "literal sense" as understood within the framework of the teaching of the fourfold sense of Scripture. This is true because, on the one hand, exegesis is not merely concerned with determining the historical informational content of biblical writings; on the other hand exegesis, in paying attention to linguistic forms

and intentions, recognizes a "dogmatic", "moral" or "eschatological" sense in many Old and New Testament texts which would have been classified as a spiritual rather than a literal sense in traditional hermeneutics.

8.5.2.2 The Theological Significance of Scholarly Exegesis

(162) Exegetical work is of fundamental importance for the church's interpretation of Scripture. Since the Bible is a book that appeared a long time ago and since the church reads the Bible as God's word in the historical words of humans, it is logical for the church to consider the *historical* interpretation of the Bible, which makes use of historical and philological methods, to be the medium for the theological interpretation of Scripture. In principle *all* questions and methods that are suitable for developing the historical meaning of biblical texts are important for the church's interpretation of Scripture. Biblical studies can only be of theological value for the church if their premises, methods and results prove their worth in the dialogue with other sciences. On the other hand, precisely their theological option and ecclesial bond help so that biblical studies are not at the mercy of rationalism or historicism, or give themselves over to sociological or psychological reductions of Scripture's meaning to particular functions, but are instead prepared for the task of historically understanding the biblical gospel.

(163) The theological significance of such scholarly interpretation of Scripture is apparent on several levels. Without the exegetical research of the Bible none of the theological disciplines could fulfill its intellectual responsibility today. The biblical sciences, working with historical-critical methods, insist that we acknowledge the historicity of the biblical testimonies to faith, see the plurality of biblical theologies, and seek the unity of Scripture in the different ways of looking at the one God and His saving action through Jesus Christ.

(164) The significance for the church's sense of faith and practice of faith lies in particular in the *critical* function which exegesis can perform. Exegesis counterbalances all attempts to appropriate Holy Scripture for social, ecclesial and personal interests which do not correspond to the testimony of the Bible. It blocks those systematizations of biblical theologies which do not do

justice to the diversity of the biblical testimonies to faith; yet it must also face the claim that the entire Bible has an inner unity which has been predetermined with the canon. Exegesis works out the difference which exists between Holy Scripture and both the historically developed forms of doctrine and the currently prevailing awareness of faith in theology and the church. In this way it provides the opportunity to call into question dominant, untested claims to validity and to prepare the ground for a productive, new encounter with Scripture.

(165) Even more important, however, is the *positive* effect which the historical interpretation of Scripture strives for. Through its historical orientation it seeks to help the faith community hear the word of God in the words of Holy Scripture as they were originally heard by the biblical authors, redactors and addressees, as far as this can be reconstructed. Particularly by means of the historical distinctions made in the interpretation of Scripture, exegesis shows the church quite clearly the great theological, spiritual and paracletic wealth to be found in the vast number and the diversity of biblical theologies. By making the dynamic correlations between historical situation and theological intent apparent, exegesis indicates which Spirit-wrought experiences support the original Christian statements of faith and how these in turn, thanks to the grace of God, open up opportunities for living which can become a revelation of perfected salvation.

8.5.2.3 The Tension between Historical and Contemporary Scriptural Interpretation

(166) The true task of exegesis is to disclose the historical sense of Scripture. At the same time the church faces the question about the *actual* binding nature of Scripture at any given time. This question cannot be answered without scholarly exegesis since the legitimacy of every normative interpretation depends on its agreement with the original sense of the biblical texts. Moreover, when exegesis is developed with the goal of being a biblical theology, it makes it possible to evaluate different theological positions as they are encountered in the Old and the New Testament within the frame of reference of the multifaceted, one, and entire Holy Scripture, i.e. *with* the Bible itself. It is only on the basis of such exegetical-theological clarification that we can

decide, in accordance with Scripture, what historical and current *legitimacy* biblical statements may claim in central questions of faith and morals.

(167) Conversely, however, exegesis cannot always establish on its own what kind of binding character particular biblical statements have for the church today. This is true not just because the faith life of the church cannot adapt itself to the research trends current at any given time. What is decisive here is that exegesis as a *historical*-theological discipline is not automatically in a position to do the job of normative interpretation with its own authentic range of questions and methodology. Its job instead is to shed light on the prevailing meaning of the texts in biblical times, not on their immediate contemporary meaning. Exegetes emphasize time and again the "unfamiliar nature" of biblical theologies and their considerable dissimilarity to the present perception of faith. We also see an important *theological* contribution in this work, and rightly so, provided it acknowledges the faith testimony of the original biblical period in its historicity and thus stresses at the same time both the temporal and the factual priority of Scripture over the post-biblical tradition of the church.

(168) Through consistent exegetical work researchers not only develop the historical sense of Scripture, but also the implicit or explicit *claim* of biblical texts that they continue to articulate the word of God. In addition biblical scholars can make apparent an inner connection between the salvific action of God attested in Sacred Scripture and the emergence of this Scripture as a document that is an original, and in this respect normative, proclamation of faith. Thus exegesis itself leads to the question of how the significance of Sacred Scripture is communicated to history and to the present moment of each era, while realizing that this question cannot be answered by exegetical means alone.

(169) All individual members, authoritative offices and fundamental actions of the church must confront the challenge of discerning the present-day relevance of Scripture. In the process they must on the one hand take into account the historical-cultural gap between the time when the Bible emerged and the present day, including the long history of the church's interpretation of Scripture. On the other hand they have to bear in mind the factual gap

between the witness to faith in Scripture, which has, by virtue of the working of the Holy Spirit, an unparalleled authority as initial, founding testimony, and today's understanding of faith which refers to this. What is necessary is not only exact historical-philological research of the Bible, but also a systematic-theological reflection on the testimony of Scripture in light of church tradition and in view of the way people understand their situations and live in the world today.

8.5.2.4 The Task of Scholarly Exegesis in the Service of the Gospel

(170) Exegesis itself must help to improve the conditions for the needed bridging of the gap to the present age. From the start it is clear that exegesis can only perform its service if it remains an interpretation of *Scripture* without any methodological or hermeneutical compromises, i.e. only if it becomes the advocate of the texts of the Bible and their message in the theological discussions of the past and present. It is just as clear that exegesis should be scriptural interpretation which is competent, relevant and in the end also comprehensible in an interdisciplinary sense. But above all it is important that exegetes actually trace theological impulses which emanate from the texts entrusted to them and take on the task of articulating the "substance", the "center", the "totality" and the "unity" of Scripture.

(171) It is of the greatest importance that exegesis and systematic theology enter into a dialogue which begins from the assumption that God's truth itself is made known in the historical form of the human words of Scripture. Only in this dialogue will it be possible to underscore the normativeness of Scripture without resorting to some sort of naive biblicism, to demonstrate the truth of biblical theology by using reasoned argument, and to present the unity of Scripture in such a way that it is capable of justifying faith theologically.

(172) A crucial task confronting the exegetical and systematic use of Scripture in view of the scriptural interpretation of the church also consists in disclosing the *spiritual* sense of Scripture in a new way: not apart from the written words of the Bible, but *in* the very letters of the texts as they were written under the conditions of a particular time and situation with a particu-

lar intention and desired effect. In this way the legitimate *concern* of the doctrine of the fourfold sense of Scripture could be accommodated under the conditions of modern thinking. The discovery of this spiritual sense of Scripture is not something that is *added* to scholarly exegesis, but is instead an essential feature of exegetical work itself. It becomes effective when we keep in mind as a matter of principle that the biblical texts arise from the working of God's Spirit and that for this reason alone they are capable of making theologically relevant statements. An exegesis which is open to the working of God's Spirit in such a way is led through the texts which are to be interpreted to the formative, historical faith experiences of the biblical authors and communities. These fundamental testimonies to faith, however, are relevant over and above the initial situation of their origin because they owe their existence to the working of the one and same Spirit who also makes Himself present in the fundamental actions of the church, especially in the Lord's Supper and in the sense of faith of the faithful, in such a way that He refers to the original biblical testimony as source and norm.

If exegetes discern the genuine spirituality of the biblical texts they have an excellent opportunity to aid in the discovery of the mystery of the living God in Jesus of Nazareth through their work on Old and New Testament scriptures.

9 The Interpretation of Scripture and the Binding Teaching of the Church

9.1 Our Starting Point and Procedure

(173) It seems that the two positions "*sola scriptura*" (we discern the truth) or "binding magisterial interpretation" (the teaching office is necessary to discern the truth) still confront each other in an unmediated way in the ordinary, denominationally influenced consciousness of believers and even occasionally in the public ecumenical debate. As a result of our discussions which have extended over many years we want to express and explain our conviction that posing as alternatives scriptural principle *or* magisterial interpreta-

tion of Scripture, the authority of the word of God *or* the authority of church office does not do justice to the position of *either* Catholics or Protestants.

(174) To provide a convincing justification for this thesis it will be necessary to treat three aspects of the question in greater detail: (1) An important foundation for all further steps towards reaching agreement is the convergence in the *determination of the relationship between Scripture and tradition* which has been attained so far and is already formulated in ecumenical documents. (2) With respect to the bearers of the transmission process we must start by explaining that all baptized people are joined together in the "*common priesthood*" and that the mandate to proclaim the gospel has been given to all of them. (3) Above all, however, our concern here is to describe the meaning of a *binding magisterial interpretation of Scripture* by church office bearers as well as by synodal or conciliar assemblies. In the course of treating these issues we will also point out those features in the denominationally determined traditions which give rise to critical questions.

(175) In each of the three sections we begin this joint attempt to formulate both our understanding of the authority of Scripture and the principles of its interpretation through binding church teaching by establishing the starting points we no longer dispute, namely the testimony of Scripture and the agreements which have already been recorded in ecumenical documents. We then describe the denominational peculiarities in the treatment of the respective factual issues which developed during the course of history. Thirdly we examine the theological content of these characteristics by referring to our shared fundamental declaration and through systematic-theological reflections which point forward.

9.2 The Biblical Understanding of Doctrine and Teaching Office – A Summary

(176) In Sacred Scripture the constant actualization and efficacious confirmation of God's saving acts are the center of life of God's people. All doctrine, in Israel as well as in the church, serves this purpose. Before we attempt in this final chapter to resolve the difficult ecumenical-theological

problems mentioned above in a fundamental way, we will first *summarize briefly in the form of theses* our shared understanding of what Sacred Scripture itself has to say concerning the central contents of its testimony and the different functions and responsibilities of the witnesses.

9.2.1 Doctrine

(177) God's saving acts in creation and for Israel are the central point of reference in Israel for all salvation-historical "remembrance", and in this context the tradition of God's commandments is the content of all teaching which is summarized in the Shema "Hear, O Israel" (Deut 6:4f.).

In Jesus' preaching we can already experience the "kingdom of God" at present as the eschatological reality of the self-revelation of the God of Israel. For this reason the teaching of Jesus to his disciples has a new revelatory quality over against the teaching tradition of the fathers. Accordingly, he himself is the only teacher of his disciples (cf. Mt 23:10), and he remains the only teacher in the entire doctrinal tradition of the post-Easter church (cf. Jn 13:13). At the same time the events of his death on the cross "for our sins" and of the raising of the crucified Messiah as the Son of God are the central message of salvation (the gospel, "the good news") which is proclaimed to all people and taught in the church (cf. 1 Cor 15:1–11).

(178) The church acquired the decisive foundation of its teaching in the fixed arrangement of the four Gospels with the apostolic writings in the New Testament: "The Lord" as the only savior of all mortals (Acts 4:12) is their sole teacher, and "the apostles" are his witnesses for all time. In the division of the canon of Sacred Scripture into two parts, the salvation-historical connection of the gospel of Christ with the history of God's saving acts for Israel and thus the identity of the God of Israel with the God of Jesus have become normative for all doctrinal traditions of the church.

(179) In the New Testament baptism in the name of Jesus Christ is the permanent point of reference of the confession of faith and the obedience of faith of all Christians. Just as the instruction for catechumens aims at their receiving Christ Jesus the Lord and living their lives in him (cf. Col 2:6), so

is the entire doctrinal tradition of the early church in all aspects of faith and life also based on the authority of the one living God in Jesus Christ, the one risen Lord, through the one life-creating Spirit of God.

At the beginning of Christianity "Scripture" (now the Old Testament) was, as the sole written testimony of revelation besides the oral apostolic tradition, the central component of both the language of religious service and the teaching of the early church. In the second century it remained a canonical authority despite all the opposition put up by individual communities and theologians (in particular Marcion).

The "illuminating" power of all doctrine as well as of the entire life of the church is the Holy Spirit (cf. 1 Cor 2:4f.; 2 Cor 4:18; Eph 1:13f.; 1 Thess 4:1–8; Jn 14:16f, 16:13–15; Acts 2:38–42).

9.2.2 The Teaching Office

(180) From early on there were teaching offices in the primitive church which were responsible for and gifted with the faithful preservation of the authoritative tradition of the apostles and prophets (Eph 2:20) and the continuation of it in such a way that it remained current: evangelists (as missionary preachers), pastors (as leaders of communities) and teachers (especially as bearers of catechetical instruction and, from the second century on, also as heads of schools). They all contributed to the spiritual "building up" of the church (Eph 4:11f.), and in actual fact they continued the work of the apostles.

(181) From the very beginning there were differences of opinion – some profound – among the early Christian teaching authorities which at times jeopardized the agreement on doctrinal tradition that was necessary for church unity. Such dissent even erupted between apostles (cf. Gal 2:11–21), as well as within the young communities (cf. 1 Cor 1–4). The so-called Council of the Apostles in Jerusalem (cf. Gal 1:1–10) became a model for discussions of doctrine aimed at restoring unity (cf. Acts 15). In the post-apostolic period doctrinal differences deepened, becoming doctrinal antitheses which led to necessary differentiations from and battles against heresies.

This required the concentration of ecclesial teaching authority in the office of the bishops by laying claim to the teaching commission and teaching authority of the apostles. This episcopal office evolved at the end of the New Testament period (cf. Acts 20:25–31; 1 Tim 3:1–16; 2 Tim 1:6–14, 2:14–26, 3:10–4:5; Tit 1:5–16 as well as the letters of Bishop Ignatius) and rapidly gained universal acceptance in the second century. It endeavored to preserve the unity of the church internally while targeting heresies externally.

(182) In their various functions and responsibilities the early church offices of preaching and teaching were thus of pivotal importance right from the start for "building up" the faith community. Whereas the Christian community during the period of the apostolic beginnings was concerned with the initial, fundamental preaching of the gospel and the establishment of local churches in many regions around the Mediterranean from its base in Jerusalem, the second and third generations were confronted with the task of preserving the correct proclamation and teaching of the gospel as well as the task of developing appropriate ecclesial authorities in order to find forms for passing on the faith. From these forms the worship and spiritual life of Christians, the canon of Scripture and the rule of faith of the church, as well as forms of ecclesial office on the local and church-wide levels were then able to evolve later on.

9.3 Holy Scripture as the Sole Criterion for Proclamation and Tradition as the Location for Attaining Certitude

9.3.1 Our Shared Convictions

(183) Our shared fundamental conviction is: "Sacred Scripture contains the whole truth of faith necessary for salvation and makes it possible for this truth to be understood as such. Since it is sufficient in a material sense, it can function as a criterion for the gospel-conformity of all church proclamation and the entire life of the church."[92] At the same time we agree that "Scrip-

---

92 *Verbindliches Zeugnis I* (note 37), p. 386 ["Joint Statement," part III, section 1 ("Ecumenical Convergences"), 1.1].

ture, which became canonical after evolving in a long transmission process in the sphere of the church, is itself a form of tradition, namely the form of apostolic proclamation, including its foundations in the writings of the Old Testament, which remains authoritative."[93]

(184) The *writings of the New Testament* mention the indispensable significance of *paradosis* as guaranteeing a life for the believing community that is true to its origins. At the same time, however, it is clear that there were already "traditions" in the apostolic period which obscured the will of God revealed in Jesus Christ. The criterion for the true *paradosis* is therefore its discernible and verifiable foundation in the authority of the incarnate Word of God.

When considering questions of doctrine, liturgy and ethics Paul frequently cites in his epistles the "tradition" preceding him (cf. 1 Cor 15; Gal 1; Rom 6) whose validity is established through the proof of its origin in Christ (cf. 1 Cor 11:23 in the context of the tradition of the Lord's Supper). In the Lucan writings there is also the clear concern to describe the teaching of the apostles in its continuity with the preaching of Jesus (cf. Lk 1:1–4; Acts 1:8, 21f., 20:17–35).

(185) The necessity to view *paradosis* critically and to distinguish between the permanently valid tradition which is justified through its divine origin, on the one hand, and the traditions created by humans which are to be given up, on the other hand, is expressed in the gospels as well as the epistles of the New Testament. In Mark (ch. 7) the tradition of the pharisees appears as a *paradosis* of humans, "the tradition of the elders," and as incompatible with the will of God which is expressed in the Torah and in the writings of the prophets. The Letter to the Colossians (2:8) contrasts the *paradosis* of humans ("human tradition") which is wrong teaching with the *paradosis* "according to Christ," true teaching. In 2 Peter (1:20f.) the authority of Scripture is attributed to its origin in the working of the Spirit of God; hence an interpretation of Scripture done on one's own authority is inadmissable. The Jo-

---

93 Ibid., p. 388 ["Joint Statement," part III, section 1 ("Ecumenical Convergences"), 1.2].

hannine texts also argue from a pneumatological perspective with respect to the question of how the truth of tradition can be recognized: The Spirit will guide us into all truth and preserve the Christian community in the truth (cf. Jn 14:17, 16:13; cf. also 2 Tim 1:14). This truth is the teaching which has been valid "from the beginning" and is authorized by apostolic witnesses who have seen and heard (1 Jn 1:1–3, 2:7,24, 3:11; 2 Jn 5f.).

(186) In the *ecumenical declarations* already available the exclusive normativeness of the testimony of Scripture for the church's proclamation of the gospel is emphasized quite clearly. This basic assertion is in no way contradicted when these ecumenical declarations and statements stress at the same time the indispensable function of church tradition in the actualization of the gospel.

(187) The document "The Gospel and the Church" (The Malta Report, 1972) placed the long-standing polemical question about the relationship between Scripture and tradition on a new foundation which has also proven to be solid in more recent rounds of dialogue[94]: "The Scripture can no longer be exclusively contrasted with tradition, because the New Testament itself is the product of primitive tradition. Yet as the witness to the fundamental tradition, Scripture has a normative role for the entire later tradition of the church."[95] The Old Testament as well should be seen in itself as the result of a tradition process which covered a long period of time. Through the canonization of the scriptures of Israel and the apostolic writings and their collection in the one Bible of the Christians the early church "placed itself under the norm of the word of God which had been given to it. It is true of all of Holy Scripture that, according to our shared conviction, it is the *norma normans non normata*; its interpretation must be the soul of the entire proclamation and the entire praxis of the church."[96]

---

94 Cf. Lutheran – Roman Catholic Joint Commission, ed., *Church and Justification* (note 32), especially no. 46, p. 33f.
95 "The Malta Report" (note 31), no. 17, quoted in: H. Meyer et al., *Dokumente wachsender Übereinstimmung*, vol. 1 (note 27), p. 253.
96 Bilateral Study Group of the German Bishops' Conference and the United Evangelical-Lutheran Church of Germany, ed., *Kirchengemeinschaft in Wort und Sakrament*, Paderborn, Hannover 1984, p. 18.

(188) "We jointly teach the unparalleled and irreplaceable authority of Holy Scripture."[97] "For us it is God's word since the witness of the prophets and apostles to whom God entrusted His word is validly brought together in it."[98] According to the Holy Scriptures themselves, God's making Himself known, His word to us, is "the comprehensive reality of God's turning to the world as its creator, judge and savior.... In the center of God's revelation in words is the Son, the one who was crucified and raised from the dead. He himself is God's Word from all eternity and as a historical person in whom the judging and recreating work of the triune God attains its goal."[99] The proclamation of this universal salvific work of God in the history of Israel and in the destiny of Jesus of Nazareth, the gospel of God's saving grace, is not just talk about salvation; rather this very occurrence of proclamation is itself a salvation event since "what God has done for the salvation of the world in Jesus Christ is transmitted in the gospel and made present in the Holy Spirit."[100] According to our shared faith, this word of God for the salvation of the world is announced in Scripture "in all its parts, in the law, in prophecy and in the praise of the psalms as well as in the gospel of the apostles."[101]

(189) The word of God which is attested in Holy Scripture and has been handed down is "both the foundation and mission of the church.... In this respect the church continues to be a creation of the word (*creatura verbi*) and at the same time a servant of the word ('*ministra verbi* ') entrusted to it. As its foundation and as its mission the word of God stands above the church."[102] It follows that all instruction in the faith as interpretation of Holy Scripture "can only be service of the word and ... not master of the word of the Lord."[103] Official, authorized proclaiming is also rooted in the prior and

---

97   Ibid.
98   Ibid., p. 17.
99   Ibid., p. 16f.
100 "The Malta Report" (note 31), no. 16, quoted in: H. Meyer et al., *Dokumente wachsender Übereinstimmung*, vol. 1 (note 27), p. 253.
101 *Kirchengemeinschaft in Wort und Sakrament* (note 96), p. 18.
102 Ibid., p. 20.
103 "The Malta Report" (note 31), no. 21, quoted in: H. Meyer et al., *Dokumente wachsender Übereinstimmung*, vol. 1 (note 27), p. 254.

preeminent hearing of the word which is, as an exhortation of the gospel, for every hearer both a call to repent and a judgment on the standards of this world (cf. Rom 12:2). Especially "where the church refuses this obedience in a concrete situation, the word of God also opposes it in a critical way"[104]: whenever its doctrines forsake the base of their apostolic foundation, whenever its lifestyle contravenes the commandments of God, and whenever its forms of piety replace the faith which trusts in God. In its incomparable normativeness which is rooted in the absolute reliability of the divine word, Holy Scripture guides us on our path of faith, shows us where we have gone astray, and calls us to repent.

9.3.2 Denominational Characteristics

(190) Historical challenges which were perceived differently produced specific, denominationally-determined emphases and ways of speaking when the relationship between Scripture and tradition was determined.

9.3.2.1 Protestant Theology

(191) *Protestant Theology* has expressed the shared fundamental conviction of the unique status of the Bible with the principle *sola scriptura*. This formula was *subjected to various misunderstandings* in the controversial theological discussions of past centuries, and it still remains vulnerable at present. Correctly understood *sola scriptura* is concerned with the binding of the faith and teaching of the church to the Old Testament witness to God and to the apostles' witness to Christ which empower one to give Christian witness today.[105]

(192) The formula *sola scriptura* would be misunderstood if it were seen as opposing the "tradition" taking place in the proclamation of Christ and thus as opposing the original apostolic tradition. What it rejects is only the addi-

---

104 *Kirchengemeinschaft in Wort und Sakrament* (note 96), p. 21.
105 Cf. G. Ebeling,"'Sola Scriptura' and Tradition," in: idem, *The Word of God and Tradition: Historical Studies Interpreting the Divisions of Christianity*, translated by S. H. Hooke, Philadelphia 1968, pp. 102–147, notes pp. 238–254.

tion of content foreign to the apostolic gospel. *The New Testament did not exist as a book at the beginning* of Christian discipleship and the commencement of the life of the first Christian community. *Instead there was the proclamation of the gospel* about God's mighty deeds in Jesus Christ which occurred through the oral preaching of those who followed him as well as in the missionary zeal and life testimony of the apostles, prophets and teachers of the first communities. The emerging New Testament scriptures were the manifestation of the proclamation event which preceded them and then continued to take place with their help.

(193) The principle of *sola scriptura* would also be misinterpreted if it were associated with giving fundamental priority to the written gospel over the orally proclaimed gospel. It is *not* the *written nature* of the word of God which matters, but the original form of the apostolic gospel which is only preserved in Holy Scripture. In antiquity and during the Middle Ages the status of oral teaching as the "*excellentior modus doctrinae*"[106] was definitely acknowledged. Martin Luther assimilated this view with respect to the proclamation of the gospel (cf. for instance *Werke. Kritische Gesamtausgabe* {"Weimarer Ausgabe"}, Weimar, 1883ff., 10, 1,1; 625,19–627,3). He also certainly regarded the fact that apostolic preaching was recorded in writing as a providential event in view of the history of the transmission of the faith. Holy Scripture is the medium through which the divine assurance of God's fidelity and reliability can reach the ears of the generations of all nations in unadulterated, pure tones. Nonetheless it belongs to the essence of this divine word passed down through human witnesses that time and again its written version becomes the preached word in the realm of the congregation and before the ears of the hearers. *Hence sola scriptura "is only rightly understood when it is referred back to the event of preaching from which Scripture comes and points to the event of preaching which is Scripture's objective."*[107]

---

106 Thomas Aquinas, *ST* III, q. 42, a. 4.
107 G. Ebeling, "'Sola Scriptura' and Tradition" (note 105), p. 112. [The English quoted above is not from this English edition of Ebeling's book, but is a direct translation of the original German in order to better capture the meaning of Ebeling's statement.]

(194) In the context of this event of preaching as the real "oral tradition" from the earliest beginnings up to today, the most valuable record of apostolic origin and its transmission is the canon of Holy Scripture itself. The canon is therefore interwoven into the faith and life of the church in a unique way. Thus, on the one hand the opposition between Scripture (as saving and judging word of God) and the church (as the creation of this divine word), which has already been emphasized and remains important, is valid. On the other hand a close relationship between Scripture and the church results from the nature of the gospel in the sense "that the content of Scripture has not been transmitted by 'mere Scripture', but rather through the spoken word of preaching, addressed therefore to the Church and borne witness to by the Church."[108] If this *union of scriptural authority, the living transmission of the gospel through its proclamation, and the church as bearer and receiver of this proclamation* is seen correctly then the formula *sola scriptura* need not be controversial.

(195) The question about what the expression *claritas scripturae* means in the Protestant theological tradition requires individual attention. Here we are concerned with the specific character and "factual authority of the content of the Bible"[109] that is clear from the words of Scripture themselves, and thus with that evident nature of the central meaning of Scripture which faith presupposes by hearing the gospel as the word of God. Luther *differentiated here between the external and the internal clarity* of Scripture. External clarity concerns the matter of Scripture which emerges "clearly" from its words; internal clarity, however, pertains to our being convinced internally of this content, a conviction which is effected in the hearts by the Holy Spirit, overcoming the *obscuritas* of human hearts. External clarity does not mean that the central content of Scripture is immediately evident to every reader in spite of that reader's prejudices or biases. For this reason Luther states that the *exposition of the external clarity* is *entrusted to the "ministerium verbi"*

---

108 Ibid., p. 134.

109 G. Wenz, "Das Schriftprinzip im gegenseitigen ökumenischen Dialog zwischen den Reformationskirchen und der römisch-katholischen Kirche: Eine Problemskizze," in: H. H. Schmid and J. Mehlhausen, ed., *Sola Scriptura: Das reformatorische Schriftprinzip in der säkularen Welt*, Gütersloh 1991, p. 313.

(cf. *Werke. Kritische Gesamtausgabe* {"Weimarer Ausgabe"}, Weimar, 1883ff., 10, 609). The proclamation or preaching of the gospel reveals the central content, the "matter" of Scripture from its words, but in such a way that "common sense" (*sensus communis*) sees clearly that this is in fact the "matter" of the words of Scripture (cf. *Werke. Kritische Gesamtausgabe* {"Weimarer Ausgabe"}, Weimar, 1883ff., 18, 656). The internal conviction that this is the content, however, does not follow from this automatically; rather *this internal clarity is wrought in the hearts by the Holy Spirit.*

(196) Luther developed his theory of the clarity of Scripture in his dispute with Erasmus in order to counter the opinion that the statements of Scripture are ambiguous and thus in need of an authoritative interpretation. His assertion that Scripture is unambiguous in and of itself had to pertain first and foremost to its external clarity. The principle did not refer to isolated, individual words, but to the clarity of the matter of Scripture as a whole which finds specific expression in each of the individual words. Even to this day there is controversy in Protestant theology as to whether the external clarity of Scripture concerns the meaning derived from its wording, which is how Johann Salomo Semler later interpreted Luther's scriptural doctrine, or whether Luther's reference to the *ministerium verbi* which is entrusted with discovering the explanation of the meaning denotes that only the proclamation of the gospel is capable of discovering and conveying this actual meaning.[110] In any case, however, the theory concerning the clarity of Scripture implies that the meaning of Scripture is to be extracted from Scripture itself as this is presupposed for its functioning as a criterion for the authenticity of church teaching.

(197) Finally, for a proper understanding of the principle of *sola scriptura* in Protestant theology and in the Protestant church it must be kept in mind that

---

110 Concerning this see on the one hand W. Pannenberg, "Was ist eine dogmatische Aussage?" in: idem, *Grundfragen systematischer Theologie*, Göttingen 1967, 3rd edition 1979, pp. 159–180, esp. p. 163f.; see on the other hand F. Beißer, *Claritas scripturae bei Martin Luther*, Göttingen 1966, pp. 82–97 and pp. 104–108, but also B. Lohse, *Luthers Theologie in ihrer historischen Entwicklung und ihrem systematischen Zusammenhang*, Göttingen 1995, pp. 211-213, esp. p. 213.

proclamation and teaching are bound to the creeds of the church. In the regional Protestant churches of Germany the creeds or confessions of the early church and the Reformation belong, along with Holy Scripture, to the foundations which establish these churches; they are enshrined as such in the constitutions of the churches. These foundations cannot be altered by legislation or by doctrinal decisions of the churches.

(198) As *norma normata* the creeds or confessions valid in the Protestant churches are subordinated to Holy Scripture as the *norma normans*; they should always be appraised by it and interpreted in its light.[111] On the other hand, however, the creeds themselves constitute an important orientation for interpreting Scripture both in the living proclamation of the church and in academic theology.[112] Here the creeds are not a material supplement to Holy Scripture, but have the purpose of ensuring that it is properly understood. In this sense Protestant theology recognizes a function of post-apostolic church tradition which is binding for it and for the church. Whether and to what degree the creed of the church is open to ongoing, authoritative and binding interpretation through new doctrinal decisions of the church – for example through its approval of ecumenical documents of convergence – is a question currently under consideration.

---

111 Cf. "Formula of Concord: The Comprehensive Summary," in: T. G. Tappert, ed. and trans., *The Book of Concord: The Confessions of the Evangelical Lutheran Church*, Philadelphia 1959, p. 464f.

112 Cf. Kirchenamt der EKD [Church Office of the Evangelical Church in Germany] ed., *Vom Gebrauch der Bekenntnisse: Zur Frage der Auslegung von Bekenntnissen der Kirche*, a contribution of the Division for the Theology of the Evangelical Church in Germany (EKD texts 53), no. 2: "Das Verhältnis von Schrift und Bekenntnis," Hanover 1995, p. 4f.; cf. also the Anglican – Lutheran Dialogue, "Pullach Report" (1972), no. 64, quoted in: H. Meyer et al., *Dokumente wachsender Übereinstimmung*, vol. 1 (note 27), p. 311; Baptists and Lutherans in Dialogue, "A Message to Our Churches" (1990), nos. 19–21, quoted in: J. Gros et al., *Growth in Agreement II* (note 28) p. 158f.; and Lutheran – Methodist Joint Commission, "The Church: Community of Grace: the Lutheran-Methodist Dialogue 1979–1984," no. 19, quoted in: J. Gros et al., *Growth in Agreement II* (note 28) p. 204.

9.3.2.2 Catholic Theology

(199) The view held in *Roman Catholic theology* that the transmission of the gospel takes place through *Sacred Scripture and tradition* and that both are therefore to be accepted "with the same sense of devotion and reverence" (*pari pietatis affectu ac reverentia*)[113] does not in any way intend to *call into question the unique significance of Sacred Scripture* in the events of the transmission of the gospel. Nor should this teaching be seen as a *contradiction* of Reformation talk about the recognition of truth made possible through *sola scriptura*. The Catholic doctrinal tradition explicitly includes in its considerations the fact that the medieval reform movements supported the sole normativeness of Sacred Scripture in all questions *de fide et moribus*.

(200) In the Constitution on Divine Revelation, *Dei Verbum*, the Second Vatican Council positions itself in the continuity of its own doctrinal tradition when it quotes the Tridentine "Decree of Reception of the Sacred Books and Apostolic Traditions." One variation in formulation, however, which expresses the renewed (compared to Trent) understanding of tradition does stand out here: The Constitution on Divine Revelation of the Second Vatican Council uses the word "tradition" exclusively in the singular in argumentative sections. The document is therefore not interested in church tradition*s* in addition to Sacred Scripture when it speaks of *traditio*, but in the *process of the living transmission of the gospel*, the word of God.

(201) Trent had already checked the tendency to split the *depositum fidei* in a material way (by rejecting the textual suggestion "*partim in scripturis – partim in traditionibus*" and using the more open "*et – et*"). The Second Vatican Council clearly rejected speech about Scripture and tradition as being the "two sources of revelation": There exists "a close connection ... between sacred tradition and sacred Scripture. For both of them, flowing from the same divine wellspring, ... form one sacred deposit of the word of God, which is committed to the church" (*Dei Verbum* 9f.). Although the text of the Constitution on Divine Revelation does not determine the relationship be-

---

113 Cf. *Dei Verbum* 9; Council of Trent, "Decree of Reception of the Sacred Books and Apostolic Traditions," DH 1501 [ND 210].

tween the two in a precise way (in the sense of the sufficiency of Scripture with respect to content and the modal characterization of tradition), it is still important to note that the efforts by a few Council Fathers to include a statement in the text on the necessity of supplementing Scripture in a material way with subject matter from tradition were rejected by the "Joint Theological Commission" responsible for preparing the document and were also rejected by the majority of the Council Fathers.

(202) For a correct understanding of the meaning of the statements in *Dei Verbum* 9 it is essential to note that, after emphasizing the unity of Scripture and tradition, the document gives a sort of definition of the characteristics of these two entities. It says that Scripture *is* the speech of God put down in writing. In contrast, the essence of tradition is defined by describing its function: Tradition *transmits* the word of God, but it is not the word of God: "*Sacra Scriptura est locutio Dei .... Sacra autem traditio verbum Dei ... integre transmittit*" (*Dei Verbum* 9). From this it is apparent that the last council tended toward the view designated in theological discussion as the sufficiency of Scripture in all truths of salvation.

(203) Against this background the formulation "*verbum Dei scriptum vel traditum* [the word of God, whether written or handed down]" (*Dei Verbum* 10) can also be interpreted in a way that does not contradict our joint conviction that the testimony of Scripture has its own special character. *Dei Verbum* 10 quotes from the Constitution on the Faith, "*Dei Filius*," of the First Vatican Council and understands Sacred Scripture as the most precious apostolic *traditum* and *tradendum*, as the written and transmitted word of God. Moreover, the little word *vel* is a constant reminder that, according to the linguistic usage of the Bible, *paradosis* is an event of many shapes and forms in which the writing of Sacred Scripture is of indispensable, fundamental importance, but which is not limited to this process of putting things down in writing. This is true both because scriptural formulations are time-dependent which makes it necessary for the biblical perception of God to be passed on creatively into the changing periods which follow, and because it is the nature of the gospel to address the hearer in a timely fashion. In this context it is important to recognize that the Second Vatican Council sought to retrieve this comprehensive biblical view of revelation in its expositions in the entire

second chapter of the Constitution on Divine Revelation under the heading "The Transmission of Divine Revelation" (*Dei Verbum* 7–10). Joseph Ratzinger called this biblical view "revelation's character of totality."[114] This denotes the dynamic totality of making the mystery of Christ present which "the Church, in her teaching, life and worship, ... [should hand] on to all generations" (*Dei Verbum* 8). Our understanding of the living transmission of the word of God can thus be extricated from the inadequate alternative "in writing or orally" (since this alternative articulates only one aspect) and opened to a life lived in faith through the Christological coloring and filling of the "*verbum traditum* [word handed down]."

(204) This briefly outlined idea of the living event of tradition which the community of the church itself is in its God-given exercise of faith (cf. *Dei Verbum* 8) also makes it possible to understand correctly a formulation of the Constitution on Divine Revelation of the Second Vatican Council which seemingly contradicts everything that has been said thus far: "Consequently, it is not from *sacred Scripture alone* that the Church draws her *certainty* about everything which has been revealed." (*Dei Verbum* 9). Mindful of the intense debate among the Council Fathers during the first and second sessions on the question of the material sufficiency of Scripture, the quoted formulation should be viewed as a decision in favor of the doctrinal position that tradition does not add any further content to Sacred Scripture when explicating God's revelation. Instead its singular function is to make it possible for the message of Sacred Scripture as "*viva vox evangelii*" to be heard in every generation. The function of *tradition* is therefor to take responsibility for the *process of attaining certitude* about the truth of the gospel testified in the biblical scriptures under changed constellations of experience, speech and knowledge. Hence tradition has absolutely essential significance in the formal-gnoseologic sphere, not in the material sphere.

(205) We can illustrate what this means by looking at the process of the formation of the canon of biblical scriptures. Certitude about the canonicity of individual biblical books is derived from the fundamental, church-wide act of

---

114 J. Ratzinger, "Kommentar zu *Die Verbum*," in: *Lexikon für Theologie und Kirche*, suppl. vol. 2, 2nd completely rev. edition, Freiburg 1967, p. 519.

acceptance, confirmation and transmission of these writings as the authentic words of God (cf. *Dei Verbum* 8). Accepting the canon of Sacred Scriptures as a theological entity also always means trusting the tradition borne by the Spirit. When tradition is entirely referred back to the collection of scriptures and when it witnesses to this collection as Sacred Scripture, then (the formation of the canon as a paradigmatic act of) tradition is not being understood as an independent entity in terms of content alongside Scripture (although it can of course be said in a very formal sense that this determination makes a "statement" which is not to be found in this form and as such in Scripture). Instead it is being seen as a dynamic realization of faith, given and made possible by the Holy Spirit, in which we accept, justify and are granted the certitude that precisely these books are the word of God.[115]

9.3.3 Conclusions

(206) Our search for the real issue underlying the different, denominationally determined formulae thus leads to the following conclusions: Protestant theology explains the principle of *sola scriptura* and the – not unambiguous – concept of the "self-interpretation of Scripture" as directed at the *content* of the gospel, the judging and saving message itself, which should be passed on and passed down. It rejects as a misinterpretation a purely formal understanding of the "principle of Scripture" which would exclude the necessary ecclesial transmission and interpretation of Scripture as well as the standardization of such interpretation through the creeds of the church (as a definitive form of church tradition). Catholic theology explains the phrase "Scripture and tradition" in such a way that the authoritative word of God is only given in the testimony of Scripture ("*divino afflante spiritu scripto*" ["consigned to writing under the inspiration of the divine Spirit"], *Dei Verbum* 9); tradition is described in a functional-modal way as a realization of the living transmission of this gospel ("*spiritu sancto assistente*" ["with the help of the Holy Spirit"], *Dei Verbum* 10). Catholic theology rejects as a misinterpretation a

---

115 Cf. *Verbindliches Zeugnis I* (note 37), pp. 388–397 ["Joint Statement," part III, sections 2–5]; K. Lehmann, "Die Bildung des Kanons als dogmatisches Ur-Paradigma: Zur Verhältnisbestimmung von Schrift, Überlieferung und Amt," in: Freiburger Universitätsblätter 108 (1990), 53–63.

conception of tradition as transmissions of truths apart from Sacred Scripture which "add to it" in terms of content. If this summary represents the two positions in the main and describes them appropriately – as we are convinced it does – then, in spite of different formulations, there is agreement between the churches in the matter itself.

9.4 The Overall Responsibility of the People of God as Bearers of the Faith Tradition

9.4.1 Our Shared Convictions

(207) It is our shared belief that "the Holy Spirit creates the church as a communion of believers through faith in the gospel and works through this communion"[116] in order to proclaim God's word, the promise of His faithfulness which applies to all humans, in the whole world and to teach all nations, making them disciples of Jesus Christ in baptism (cf. Mt 28:19). "According to Scripture witnessing to the word of God has been assigned to the church as a whole and to all its members."[117] We agree on the statement that all the people of God are called to witness and to serve, and that every single individual should participate in proclaiming the gospel with his or her gifts and abilities.

(208) Just as we exist as persons in our unmistakable uniqueness only within the framework of our social relationships, dependencies and obligations, so too does the God-given salvation that we receive have this individual and social structure: Our personal life of faith is integrated into the community of the people of God, imparted in it, borne by it and bound to it.

(209) The *biblical writings* attest that God revealed Himself in history through His actions for a people whose believing trust He is trying to gain. The people, the faith community, are called to acknowledge God and to bear

---

116 Lutheran – Roman Catholic Joint Commission, ed., *Church and Justification* (note 32), no. 41, p. 31f.
117 *Kirchengemeinschaft in Wort und Sakrament* (note 96), no. 14, p. 21.

witness to Him in the world. Protestant Christians as well can say with the words of the Second Vatican Council: "It has pleased God ... to make men holy and save them not merely as individuals without any mutual bonds, but by making them into a single people, a people which acknowledges him in truth and serves him in holiness" (*Lumen Gentium* 9). This consciousness characterized the faith of Israel: "And I will walk among you, and will be your God, and you shall be my people" (Lev 26:12; cf. Deut 26:17–19; Jer 24:7, 31:1, 31:33; Ezek 36:28, 37:23, 37:27). This knowledge influenced the preaching of Jesus and his efforts to gather the people together (cf. Lk 13:34). This conviction supported the post-Easter preaching of the young church. "As on earth the Lord called and gathered people by the proclamation of the 'good news of the kingdom' (Mt 4:23, 9:35, 24:14; Mk 1:14), so too after Pentecost the calling and the fresh gathering of God's people is continued by the proclamation of the 'good news of Christ' (Rom 15:19; cf. 1:16; 1,1–9)."[118]

(210) The New Testament (following Ex 19:6 and Isa 61:6) called the people chosen by God Himself to make His name known to all the nations a "royal priesthood" (1 Pet 2:9), a "holy priesthood" (1 Pet 2:5). They have been called by God to proclaim His good deeds to all: God has led us out of the darkness of death and given us the light of the life that cannot be lost (cf. 1 Pet 2:9). The honor and duty of all those who confess their Christian faith in baptism is to testify to the hope for the redeemed life of all creation, a hope grounded in God's action in Christ Jesus.

From the New Testament perspective the call and mission of all the baptized to proclaim the gospel result from the Spirit-giftedness of the entire people of God. The Old Testament prophets attest the presence of the Spirit in all maids and servants, in all the great and the small, and in the young and the old (cf. Joel 3:1–5 [Joel 2:28–32 in the NRSV]; Isa 32:15–18). In an impressive way both the early and the later texts of the New Testament have this conviction regarding the diversity of the workings of God's one Spirit in

---

118 Lutheran – Roman Catholic Joint Commission, ed., *Church and Justification* (note 32), no. 34, p. 28f.

common (cf. 1 Cor 12:4–11; Rom 12:6–8; Acts 2:17–21; Jn 15:26f.; 1 Jn 2:20, 27).

(211) The belief that all the baptized are responsible for the living transmission of the gospel has already been formulated in *ecumenical documents*. This mission of all the members of the church to bear witness is comprised of the "priesthood of all the baptized and the special church office of those called to it. It demands that God's word must be witnessed and proclaimed today in the preaching, teaching, confession and action of both the church and individual Christians."[119]

(212) "We share the conviction that the church is preserved in the truth by the word of God because the Holy Spirit, who leads the church into all truth, has been promised to it."[120] "The commission to continue in the truth, like the promise to bring this about, holds good for the church as a whole. Our churches are agreed on this. We also agree that it is primarily the Spirit of God, promised to the church and dwelling in it, who enables it so to continue and gives it the authority to distinguish truth and error in a binding way, that is, to teach. Finally, we agree that for his activity God in the Holy Spirit makes use of temporal instruments and circumstances which he himself has bestowed upon the church as a temporal and creaturely entity; and that the ministry is one of these instruments and circumstances."[121]

9.4.2 Denominational Characteristics

(213) Particularly in the medieval history of the church there were restrictions and undesirable developments with respect to this overall responsibility. In the sixteenth century the Reformation opposed these trends; contemporary Roman Catholic theology and the Roman Catholic Church of today are also trying to overcome them.

---

119 *Kirchengemeinschaft in Wort und Sakrament* (note 96), no. 14, p. 21f.
120 Ibid., no.13, p. 21.
121 Lutheran – Roman Catholic Joint Commission, ed., *Church and Justification* (note 32), no. 206, p. 100f.

(214) Following Martin Luther the *churches of the Reformation* stress the *general priesthood* of all believers and baptized persons. It is grounded in their communion with Jesus Christ which is mediated through baptism and faith and also includes participation in his priesthood. All baptized people are called to *witness* to Jesus Christ and to *pray for* and *serve* their fellow human beings. Such participation in the priesthood of Christ, however, does not include the authorization to proclaim the gospel publicly or to administer the sacraments. Every Christian and thus also the "Christian assembly or congregation" has the "right and authority" to evaluate "all teaching," to measure it by the standard of the biblical gospel. For this reason the totality of believers has an active share of the responsibility for seeing that proclamation takes place and that the teaching is "correct", i.e. in accordance with the gospel. But not every person is entitled to teach publicly. That the sheep – to use the language of John's Gospel – recognize the voice of the good shepherd in the church's proclamation does indeed presuppose that they live in his flock, are instructed by his voice and become familiar with the biblical gospel. Bestowed by the testimony of Scripture and wrought by the Spirit, the "reception" of ecclesial teaching is the way in which the church as a whole – and each baptized person in it according to his or her own gifts and calling – distinguishes between truth and error. Such reception, however, always presupposes that the proclamation of the word has taken place. In the life of the church that proclamation is entrusted in a special way to the ordained ministry. Its specific commission is to preserve the congregations in the unity of the apostolic faith in the gospel of Christ by proclaiming the gospel in the public sphere of the church.

(215) In many very fundamental and concrete declarations at the Second Vatican Council the *Roman Catholic Church* emphasized the dignity and function of the people of God and the responsibility of everyone for the gospel; it regained the biblical perspective which had to a large extent been obscured. The biblically motivated reorientation of the Council is already evident in the programmatic structure of the Dogmatic Constitution on the Church, *Lumen Gentium*. After the church is initially and decisively defined in chapter 1 ("The Mystery of the Church") as a foundation and creation of God, and prior to any individual statements, Chapter 2 ("The People of God") focuses on the fundamental characteristic which all baptized people

have in common: Christian existence as a *common priesthood* of the faithful. It is not until chapter 3 that "hierarchical office," in particular the episcopate, is looked at, before chapter 4 once again takes up the responsibility of the "laity" (those not ordained) for the entire church. Chapter 5 then considers the call of all to holiness.

(216) The Council Fathers formulated the teaching concerning the vocation of all the baptized as follows: "The holy People of God shares also in Christ's prophetic office. It spreads abroad a living witness to Him.... The body of the faithful as a whole, anointed as they are by the Holy One (cf. 1 Jn 2:20 and 27), cannot err in matters of belief" (*Lumen Gentium* 12). "The baptized, by regeneration and the anointing of the Holy Spirit, are consecrated into ... a holy priesthood (*consecrantur*)" (*Lumen Gentium* 10). "So it is that this messianic people ... (e)stablished by Christ as a fellowship of life, charity, and truth ... is also used by Him ... and is sent forth into the whole world as the light of the world and the salt of the earth (cf. Mt 5:13–16)" (*Lumen Gentium* 9). "Christ, the great prophet, who proclaimed the kingdom of His Father by the testimony of His life and the power of His words, continually fulfills His prophetic office until His full glory is revealed. He does this not only through the hierarchy who teach in His name and with His authority, but also through the laity. For that very purpose He made them His witnesses and gave them understanding of the faith and the grace of speech (cf. Acts 2:17–18; Rev 19:10)" (*Lumen Gentium* 35).

(217) The document's intentional use of the classical terms *jus et officium, munus, consecratio,* and *sacerdotium sanctum* to describe the status and the function of all the baptized consciously opened up the supposedly unambiguous terminology previously used in systematic theology and canon law for church offices. Thus it follows that the expression "teaching office of the church" denotes first of all and in principle the official commission of all Christians, "the mission of the whole Christian people" (*Lumen Gentium* 31) to bear witness to the gospel. The Catholic description of the doctrinal responsibility of the whole church also calls for a more precise determination of the relationship between the responsibility of all baptized people for church doctrine and that of the holders of the special teaching office.

9.4.3 Conclusions

(218) Against the backdrop of the practical expression and the theological accentuation of this overall responsibility of all Christians, which vary in the different denominations, our agreement concerning the function of the entire people of God in the transmission of the gospel can be *summarized* as follows:

We agree that the faithful, qualified through the "priesthood of all the baptized," have received a share in the prophetic office of Jesus Christ, are given the knowledge of faith by the Holy Spirit, are held together in the truth, and are commissioned to witness to this truth of the gospel of God.

At the same time we jointly emphasize that this "teaching ministry of the church as a whole" does not in any way stand in opposition to the special service of the church "office bearers or ministers" (in the narrow, classical sense of this phrase). The responsibility of all Christians for the genuine truth of the gospel does not exclude the specific mission of the called, ordained proclaimers and teachers of the gospel. Rather, it presupposes this just as, conversely, the special quality of the office bound to ordination is related to the general priesthood of all in a constitutive way.

9.5 "Teaching Office of the Church" – the Special Responsibility of Ordained Ministers

9.5.1 Our Shared Convictions

(219) We share the conviction that speech about the "common priesthood of all the baptized" does not yet answer the question of what specific quality and which functions befit the special church ministry. We jointly stress the service character of every office in the church. The special service of the teaching office in the church consists in reminding the church, through the power of the Holy Spirit (cf. Jn 14:26), of its salvation-historical origin, of God's action in and for Christ Jesus, and in gathering the faith community in the unity of this original, norm-giving experience.

(220) In the Old and the New Testament the *biblical scriptures* contain numerous and varied references to *teaching* and *learning*. The goal of both teaching and learning is to live according to God's directives. Moses is the great teacher for Israel (cf. Deut 4:1). The teaching of the prophets is also understood in view of the Torah (cf. Isa 1:17, 26:9f.; Jer 6:16). The book of Deuteronomy judges the authenticity of prophecy by the great commandment (cf. Deut 13:2–6 [Deut 13:1–5 in the NRSV], 18:20). On the other hand, the prophets can distinguish between God's commandments and human statutes on the basis of the Torah. The Torah is entrusted to priests, Levites and elders (cf. Deut 31:9) so that they, as individuals and collegially, can be concerned about the correct teaching of the law (cf. Neh 8:8f.; *Pirke Avot* 1). The preservation of teaching in accordance with true prophecy which the Torah interprets is the condition for the life of all the people (cf. Prov 29:18). The psalmist asks that God teach him his paths and laws (cf. Ps 25:4, 119:12). The hope for the "new covenant" also expects that no one will need human instruction any more since God Himself will have become the teacher of His people (cf. Jer 31:34; Isa 54:13).

Christians see this hope fulfilled in Jesus (cf. Jn 6:45; 1 Thess 4:9). He is the teacher for them, he alone can instruct them about the kingdom of God (cf. Mk 4:1f, 33f.; Mt 5:1f., 7:28f.; Lk 11:1; Jn 18:20). All church teaching is participation in his teaching (cf. Mt 28:20). Borne by his authority and formed by his mandate, the post-Easter witnesses as well can continue "teaching the word of God" (Acts 18:11). Teaching in the New Testament refers to the memory of Jesus in an elemental way (cf. Mt 28:19f.), especially to his death and his resurrection (cf. Acts 4:2,5:42; 28:31). The reference here to the church's *tradition of belief* is important very early on (cf. Rom 6:17; 1 Cor 11:23, 15:1–3). In the post-apostolic period the special responsibility of the (episcopal) "teachers" includes distinguishing between sound doctrine and false teaching (cf. 1 Tim 1:10, 4:6; 2 Tim 4:3; Titus 1:9, 2:1) so that the "doctrine of God our Savior" (Titus 2:10) is not distorted, but preserved and understood.

(221) According to Paul the office of teacher derives directly from the charismatic gifts in the *ecclesia* (cf. 1 Cor 12:28f.; Rom 12:7). In the late texts of the New Testament one can observe a greater institutionalization of the ec-

clesial "teaching office" (cf. Eph 2:20, 4:11f.; Acts 20:25–31; 1 Tim 3:1–16; 2 Tim 1:6–14, 2:14–26, 3:10–4:5; Titus 1:5–16) which, however, still applies to the entire community of the faithful (cf. Acts 2:38–42) and is borne by the working of God's Spirit (cf. Jn 14:16, 16:4–15; 1 Cor 2:4f.; Eph 1:13f.). In the Pauline account and (in a different way) in the Lucan account of the Council of the Apostles in Jerusalem the memory is preserved that the most important doctrinal decision in the history of Christianity was made collegially, in the interplay of "the apostles and the elders" (Acts 15:1–29), and dialogically, in the reciprocal acceptance shown between the "party from Antioch" led by Paul and Barnabas and the "party from Jerusalem" led by James, Cephas and John (cf. Gal 2:1–10).

(222) It is significant for describing the relation between the word of God and the teaching ministry of the church that the *principle of tradition* (which refers to hearing and teaching accurately) is already connected to the *principle of succession* (which refers to faithful discipleship) during the period the New Testament developed. The preservation of the content of the apostolic testimony (through the collection of the canonical writings) as the material element, and the obligation of the leaders of the congregations to interpret these writings faithfully (through the laying on of hands) as the formal element of the authentic transmission of the word of God refer to each other and apply to each other (cf. 1 Tim 4:14; 2 Tim 1:6; 1 Tim 1:18; 2 Tim 2:1f., 4:2; Tit 2:1, 2:8). Thus the "teaching office" of the ordained ministry of the church does not establish an additional authority apart from that of the word of God, but is, according to its divinely-ordained determination, the Spirit-borne agent for the binding pronouncement and reliable attestation of the word of God. Precisely because of this indissoluble intertwining and mutual interdependence of Scripture and the teaching ministry, the only criterion serving the correct interpretation of Scripture is Scripture itself insofar as the apostolic witness to God's definitive promise of Himself has taken shape in it.

(223) In *ecumenical discussions* the joint conviction has been formulated repeatedly that the church's teaching office has a responsibility with respect to the living actualization of the one gospel of God which cannot be delegated: "Just as the church has its origin and foundation in the totality of the

Christ event, so also is *the ministry of the church constituted and instituted with the saving work of Christ* (2 Cor 5:18f.) .... We agree that both of the following can be said of the special office of church ministry: It is a divine institution and therefore not the result of later delegation or commission by the church, and it stands in the midst of the church under its one Lord, Jesus Christ."[122] "In continuous relation to the normative apostolic tradition, it makes present the mission of Jesus Christ."[123] It is neither historically nor theologically a derivative of the common baptismal priesthood, the mission of all Christians to bear witness. Rather, precisely in contrast to the rest of the baptized and in pastoral service to the congregation, the exalted Lord himself as the one "acting in the present (in his Spirit), takes the minister into his service ... (as) his tool and instrument"[124]. "The presence of this ministry in the community 'signifies the priority of divine initiative and authority in the Church's existence'."[125]

(224) Notwithstanding the different historical shapes of the structures for executing the ecclesial office, it remains valid according to our conviction

---

122 *Kirchengemeinschaft in Wort und Sakrament* (note 96), no. 60, p. 65; cf. ibid., no. 75, p. 84: We "agree that the authority of the office of church ministry is founded in and limited by the mandate to preach the gospel and to administer the sacraments. The church of Jesus Christ is built up by word and sacrament. Its unity is founded in word and sacrament. The pastoral office, the service to the unity of the church gets its orientation through the preaching of the gospel and the administration of the sacraments."
123 Roman Catholic – Lutheran Joint Commission, ed., *Das geistliche Amt in der Kirche* (note 33), no. 20, p. 21.
124 Ibid., no. 21, p. 22.
125 Ibid., no. 20, p. 21; the statement quotes Accra (*Faith and Order* 1974), no. 14. Cf. ibid., nos. 23 and 24: "Inasmuch as the ministry is exercised on behalf of Jesus Christ and makes him present, it has authority over against the community. 'Whoever listens to you listens to me' (Lk 10:16). The authority of the ministry must therefore not be understood as delegated by the community. This authority of the ministry is however not to be understood as an individual possession of the minister, but it is rather an authority with the commission to serve in the community and for the community. Therefore, the exercise of the authority of the ministry should involve the participation of the whole community."

that the mandate for the authorized public preaching of the gospel – regardless of the question of each individual believer's conscience (and the *testimonium internum* in one's heart) – also includes "the obligation to oppose every falsification of the gospel"[126] since there are "many rebellious people, idle talkers and deceivers" (Tit 1:10). Ministers are designated to teach on behalf of the exalted Lord and in his authority. Consequently their support of truth and their rejection of error is confirmed by the divine Spirit. So long as they publicly express at the same time the religious conviction of the entire church community concerning the saving power of the divine word, their interpretation of the word of God has the right to be heard prior to any experiences, opinions and convictions of the individual believer. Thus it is valid to state: "It is less the teaching ministry as such which is controversial between our churches than the question of its scope and who has been entrusted with it."[127]

9.5.2 Denominational Characteristics

(225) The distinctive, denominationally determined developments with respect to the question of the binding, ecclesial interpretation of Scripture can be quite clearly discerned.

(226) In *Protestant theology* the fundamental determination of the relationship between the ordained ministry and the priesthood of baptism, a determination which is still controversial and under discussion, depends above all on one's understanding of the statements in articles 5, 7 and 14 of the *Augsburg Confession*. In a joint formulation we have already expressed our view of this relationship (and thus our interpretation) of the respective statements of the *Augsburg Confession* which we call to mind again here: "Through baptism, all Christians participate in Christ's priesthood, and together they are a single priestly people.... But the ministry of public proclamation of the gospel and the administration of the sacraments in the church (a ministry that includes a special responsibility for the unity and hence for the guidance of the congregation ...) is not entrusted to all. For this, according to the Lutheran and Re-

---

126 *Kirchengemeinschaft in Wort und Sakrament* (note 96), no. 76, p. 89.
127 Ibid., no. 76, p. 87f.

formed view ... 'a regular call' (*Augsburg Confession*, art. 14 ...; cf. *Apology of the Augsburg Confession*, art. 14 ...) ... is required.... The ordained ministry cannot be traced back to the congregation. It has its origin in a divine commission and institution (*Augsburg Confession*, art. 5 ...)."[128] Accordingly, on the basis of this specific divine commission "the ministry, along with its mission and authority to preach the gospel and inseparably from them, is given a responsibility for the 'purity' of the proclaimed gospel and the 'right' administration of the sacraments 'according to the Gospel'."[129] From its approach, therefore, Reformation thinking "does not lead ... into a depreciation, far less a rejection, of binding church teaching and of a teaching ministry of the church."[130]

(227) In the history of the Reformation churches, responsibility for unity in the teaching of the gospel which went beyond the local churches found its expression above all through the formation of the confessions and the validity of the catechisms. Moreover, Lutheran teaching is familiar with the regional office of bishop which has the supervision of teaching as one of its fundamental functions (*Augsburg Confession*, art. 28). Since the Catholic bishops (with few exceptions) could not be won over to the Reformation in Germany in the 16th century, the Reformers found other forms of regional episcopé [pastoral supervision] such as superintendents and church government by the territorial sovereign. The office of bishop itself was retained in some Lutheran churches outside Germany (e.g. in Sweden), and there were isolated attempts in Germany to reinstall it. In the Reformed churches responsibility for the regional guidance of the churches was delegated to synods.

(228) Since the 19th century synods have become a fundamental institution of regional church administration in the church constitutions of German Protestant churches. Today the majority of members are non-ordained parishion-

---

[128] K. Lehmann and W. Pannenberg, ed., *The Condemnations of the Reformation Era* (note 36), p. 148.
[129] Lutheran – Roman Catholic Joint Commission, ed., *Church and Justification* (note 32), no. 208, p. 101.
[130] Ibid., no. 215, p. 104.

ers who take part in the governing of the church on the regional as well as the local level. The synodal office of bishop (territorial or regional bishop) was created more recently in Germany. The question of whether responsibility for doctrine behooves the synods is answered differently by the church constitutions. In reality synods exercise such responsibility for doctrine which then often has the form of a majority decision. The tension between this practice and the provision of article 14 of the *Augsburg Confession* has not been resolved. According to this article the public proclamation of doctrine is reserved to the ordained ministry in the church. In the Protestant churches the Leading Clergy (and also collegial governing committees) actually do have a special responsibility for doctrine, together with the synods, as well as in contrast to them. This responsibility, however, should be made even more prominent and important through the collegial responsibility of all the ordained as well as of theological teachers and faculties.

(229) Doctrinal decisions also have a *binding character* in the Protestant churches through their having been received by the church. The example of the Theological Declaration of Barmen demonstrates this, but it is also discernible in the case of the Reformation creeds or confessions. Especially with respect to these it is clear that there can even be a legal sanctioning of this kind of binding character (cf. above, 9.3.2.1). That does not set aside the conviction that, according to Protestant understanding, all binding teaching should be viewed ever anew in the light of Holy Scripture and that for this reason there is an ultimate "reservation as to that binding character" or "binding nature" which cannot be dispelled.[131]

(230) With regard to the task of safeguarding the unity of the entire church on the basis of the gospel, the Reformation tradition looked to the example of the general councils of the early church. Already in the 19th century, but especially in the 20th century world-wide alliances of church denominations and the World Council of Churches have been formed. A future goal is to strive for a communion of different churches under various models of unity. In their dialogue with the Roman Catholic church Lutheran theologians have

---

131 Cf. ibid., no. 222, p. 108; no. 228, p. 110.

also not ruled out the "office of the papacy as a visible sign of the unity of the churches ... insofar as it is subordinated to the primacy of the gospel by theological reinterpretation and practical restructuring."[132] In the current discussion in the Protestant churches, however, it is still open what concrete shape such a church-wide Petrine ministry could take.

(231) According to *Catholic tradition* it would be a limitation of the "teaching ministry of the church" to simply identify it with the teaching authority of ordained office bearers. There are different forms of participation in the teaching ministry of the church. Not only did emperors convene councils, preside over them, and enforce their decrees, or princes and theologians take part and vote in them in earlier centuries. According to canon 339 of the *Codex of Canon Law* it is also possible for non-bishops to be appointed to take part in an ecumenical council. All priests are *cooperatores* of the bishops; like these they have as their "primary duty the proclamation of the gospel of God to all" ("*Presbyteri utpote Episcoporum cooperatores, primum habent officium Evangelium Dei omnibus evangelizandi*": *Presbyterorum Ordinis* 4; cf. *Lumen Gentium* 25). The Second Vatican Council states explicitly that pastors in particular should also invoke the help of the laity in the practical exercise of their "*munus magisterii*" [teaching office] (*Christus Dominus* 30). All "lay people" who have had a theological education and work in the parishes with official authorization and a canonical mission ("*missio canonica*") or who are involved in passing on the faith in schools and theological universities teach the faith of the church publicly and by virtue of their "office".[133] It thus makes sense to speak of a "structured

---

132 "The Malta Report" (note 31), no. 66, quoted in: H. Meyer et al., *Dokumente wachsender Übereinstimmung*, vol. 1 (note 27), p. 266.
133 This statement is reinforced when we recall the medieval distinction between a "*magisterium cathedrae pastoralis*" of the bishops and a "*magisterium cathedrae magistralis*" of the professors of theology: "Insofar as the Latin term '*magisterium*' definitely also denotes the academic teaching of those who have acquired a master's or doctor's degree, talking about a teaching office of theologians is based on indisputably legitimate usage.... The neo-scholastic textbooks at the beginning of this century usually distinguish between an 'authentic', i.e. public and authoritative teaching office of the bishops and an 'academic' teaching office of scholars. In the texts of the Second Vatican Council only the former, namely the 'authentic' teaching

teaching ministry" when viewing the Catholic theological tradition. The role and authority of the bishops can only be correctly understood in the context of the entire people of God and in cooperation with the teachers of faith who are also active in an official capacity.

(232) The Second Vatican Council emphasizes that the bishops are "authentic teachers, that is, teachers endowed with the authority of Christ" (*Lumen Gentium* 25). The Council harks back to the original meaning of the word authentic (i.e. "reliable, guaranteeing genuineness"), disregarding that – not unequivocal – usage adopted in Catholic theology which had contrasted "authentic" with "infallible" in the sense that a statement is not infallible, but ("only") authentic, that is, valid insofar as and as long as it is well founded in the matter itself. Behind this conceptual distinction between "infallible" and "authentic" lies the experience that there are doctrinal statements which themselves claim to be ("only") authentic teaching, i.e. they might have to be corrected, so they are perhaps not free from error. In 1967 in their still very useful "Letter to All Who Have Been Commissioned by the Church to Proclaim the Faith" the German bishops stated the following: "With respect to error and the possibility of error in non-defined doctrinal statements of the church ... we should first of all see in a realistic and resolute manner that, in general, humans must also always live their lives 'to the best of their knowledge and belief' on the basis of perceptions which are, on the one hand, not known to be absolutely certain theoretically, and yet should be respected as valid norms for thinking and acting 'here and now' since they cannot be re-

---

office, plays a role while the latter remains unmentioned. Nevertheless, precisely this twofold use of the expression 'teaching office' can be helpful when we are concerned with clarifying the different functions which come into play here." (A. Dulles, "Lehramt und Unfehlbarkeit," in: W. Kern, H. J. Pottmeyer, M. Seckler, ed., *Handbuch der Fundamentaltheologie*, vol. 4, Freiburg 1988, pp. 153–178, quote p. 162). Regarding the history of the term "magisterium" cf. also: Y. Congar, "Pour une histoire sémantique du terme 'magistère'," in: *Revue des sciences philosophiques et théologiques* 60 (1976) 85–98; idem, "Bref historique des formes du 'magistère' et de ses relations avec les docteurs," in: *Revue des sciences philosophiques et théologiques* 60 (1976) 99–112; see also I. Riedel-Spangenberger, "Verkündigungsdienst und Lehrautorität der Kirche," in: W. Aymans et al., ed., *Juri Canonico Promovendo*: Festschrift for H. Schmitz, Regensburg 1994, 153–174.

vised for the time being.... Even the church in its teaching and praxis cannot always and in each case be compelled to choose between either making a conclusively binding doctrinal decision or simply remaining silent and leaving everything up to the arbitrary opinion of the individual. To safeguard the real and ultimate substance of faith it must make doctrinal pronouncements, even at the risk of an occasional error, which carry a certain degree of obligation and yet, since they are not a definition of faith, also have a certain provisional nature about them, up to the possibility of error. There is no other way that the church can proclaim or interpret its faith as a defining reality of life and apply it to each new human situation."[134]

(233) "The task of authentically interpreting the word of God ... has been entrusted exclusively to the living teaching office of the Church" ("*munus authentice interpretandi verbum Dei ... soli vivo ecclesiae magisterio concreditum est,*" *Dei Verbum* 10). This declaration of Vatican II is in part a word-for-word adoption of a statement from Pius XII's encyclical *Humani generis* (1950) which had emphasized in a strictly antithetical formulation[135] the priority of the responsibility of the universal church over a (possible) participation of individuals. Vatican II places the emphasis differently by inserting the quote where the community of the entire holy people and the harmony between the faithful and leaders are confirmed, thus determining the direction for understanding the phrase *soli magisterio* which is in many respects integrated and thus also "restricted": "so that in holding to, practicing and professing the heritage of the faith, there results on the part of the bishops and faithful a remarkable common effort" (*Dei Verbum* 10). The phrase *soli magisterio* articulates the juridical aspect of the validity, i.e. of the "binding character" of an action that acquires its importance and its "inerrancy" from the promise of the Spirit which is directed to the entire faith community: "*ea*

---

134 *Schreiben der Deutschen Bischöfen an alle, die von der Kirche mit der Glaubensverkündigung beauftragt sind,* Trier 1967, p. 12f.
135 "*Quod quidem depositum nec singulis christifidelibus nec ipsis theologis divinus Redemptor concredit authentice interpretandum, sed soli ecclesiae magisterio.*" (Pius XII, *Humani generis,* DH 3886 [ND 859: "The task of interpreting the deposit authentically was entrusted by our divine Redeemer not to the individual Christian, nor even to the theologians, but only to the Church's teaching authority."].

infallibilitate pollere, qua divinus Redemptor ecclesiam suam ... instructam esse voluit" (DH 3074 [ND 839, the First Vatican Council's Dogmatic Constitution on the Church, *Pastor aeternus*: "the infallibility with which the divine Redeemer willed his church to be endowed"]).

(234) When exercising their teaching ministry the bishops are referred to the diachronic and synchronic consensus of the church which they should attest, safeguard and, if necessary, make apparent by defending it.[136] This was also the view of Melchior Cano who, in his *Loci theologici*, recalls the doctrinal position of the early church. According to this position the whole church is the actual bearer of tradition, and the bishops, whose service is the transmission of the faith of the whole church, are bound to the faith of the whole church in their decisions.[137] The teaching office should convey the gospel entrusted to the entire church, articulate the faith of the whole church in a representative manner, and protect it from falsification. This office is a ministry in the church and for the church. As an official speaker at the First Vatican Council, Bishop Gasser explained the conviction that binding (papal) doctrinal decisions need to be reconnected to the perception of faith of the entire church and to the agreement on faith with the entire church. Among other statements, this thought is reflected in the following formulations of the Constitution on the Church, *Pastor aeternus*: "(T)he Roman Pontiffs ..., sometimes by calling together ecumenical Councils or sounding out the mind of the Church throughout the world, sometimes through regional Councils, or sometimes by using other helps ... have defined as having to be held those matters which, with the help of God, they had found consonant with the Holy Scripture and with the apostolic Tradition. For the Holy Spirit was not promised to the successors of Peter that they might disclose a new doctrine by his revelation, but rather, that, with his assistance, they might jealously guard and faithfully explain the revelation or deposit of faith that was handed down through the apostles" (DH 3069 and 3070 [ND 835 and 836]).

---

136 Cf. H. Pottmeyer, "Normen, Kriterien und Strukturen der Überlieferung," in: W. Kern, H. J. Pottmeyer, M. Seckler, ed., *Handbuch der Fundamentaltheologie* (note 133), p. 143.
137 Cf. M. Cano, *De Locis theologicis* IV, 4.

(235) Just like the formulation "*soli magisterio concreditum*" of the Second Vatican Council,[138] talk at the First Vatican Council of the "irreformable" doctrinal decisions of the Bishop of Rome "*ex sese et non ex consensu ecclesiae*" (DH 3074 [ND 839: "of themselves, not because of the consent of the Church"]) is to be understood in the juridical sense. At that time the sentence was directed against particular forms of conciliarism and Gallicanism; its intention is to exclude each and every *legal authority* above the pope. By contrast, this in no way means that the pope could declare a doctrine infallible which has not been attested as true by the consensus of the whole Spirit-directed church. A legal protection of papal doctrinal decisions, for instance through a formal procedure of approval, is declared to be unnecessary. The Bishop of Rome is deemed to be capable of knowing the church-wide consensus of faith whose origin and distinct moment in time are grounded in the working of the Spirit of God.

(236) The function of the entire church in the faithful transmission of the gospel consists above all in "steadfastness" (*perseveratio*; cf. *Dei Verbum* 10). From their steadfast faithfulness to their origin in God's action the people of God acquire the certainty that they can get through the present and win the future. This is because the biblical term *hupomone* (patience, endurance: Rom 12:12; 1 Cor 13:7; Heb 10:32,36; James 1:12) is not a plea to cling to the past or a plea for immobility or resignation, but the strength to walk the arduous path into what is open and unexpected and to link daily confidence to the promise of what is to come. With respect to the relationship of the faithful to the binding statements of the teaching office this also always means that the individual's personal life of faith is the location where the truth of doctrine is recognized and experienced in that it must "get across"

---

138 Cf. Y. Congar, "Towards a Catholic Synthesis," in: J. Moltmann and H. Küng, ed., M. Lefébure, Eng. lang. ed., *Concilium* (1981 / 8: *Who Has the Say in the Church?*), Edinburgh, New York ,1981, pp. 68–80, esp. 76f.: "The word authority is here [*Dei Verbum* 10; *Lumen Gentium* 25] taken in a juridical sense .... We do not, unfortunately, to our knowledge have a monograph on the precise sense and uses of this term in ecclesiology .... *(I)t is clear that the recognition of this truth is not a monopoly of the body of bishops.* The latter cannot be isolated from the whole Church ...."

and prove itself here.[139] According to classical Catholic tradition which can cite Augustine and Thomas Aquinas, this decisive confirmation by the conscience of the believer is of such fundamental importance that, in case of a serious conflict, he or she would ultimately have to follow his or her conscience and not what the teaching office says.

(237) Finally with regard to the magisterium's pronouncements of binding teaching we should address the concern on the Protestant side that these pronouncements are "so objectivized in specific ecclesial components that they appear to be exempt from critical questioning," although "in the Catholic view these ecclesial offices and decisions have their historically variable forms and are carried out by sinful human beings. For that reason they continue to be imperfect, can obscure the indestructible holiness of the church and therefore are in need of reform."[140]

(238) Current Catholic theology,[141] supported by diverse, concrete experiences in the history of faith, is convinced that "conclusively binding" does not mean timeless or unchanging. Councils "overtake" one another, complement, correct and reread old texts, place different emphases, put things in new contexts, change the linguistic forms and reconnect to Sacred Scripture

---

139 "The general belief that God's own word is expressed in the medium of church teaching does not, namely, invalidate the theological principle that God's word can only be legitimated by the *testimonium spiritus sancti*, just as belief in Scripture as God's word does not result in an 'external scriptural authority' in the sense that a saying of Scripture is already justified before one's conscience as God's word by its being written in Scripture. In this respect Catholic theology can state without questioning the authority of Scripture or the authority of the magisterium that the highest authority of humans is their conscience as the place where God's word is heard and the working of the Spirit is experienced." (G. Hintzen, "Die Selbstbezeugung des Wortes Gottes: Gedanken zu Schrift, Tradition und kirchlichem Lehramt," in: *Catholica* {1990} 1–25, quote on p. 10).
140 Cf. Lutheran – Roman Catholic Joint Commission, ed., *Church and Justification* (note 32), nos. 160 and 161, p. 84.
141 Cf. among others D. Wiederkehr, "Das Prinzip der Überlieferung," in: W. Kern, H. J. Pottmeyer, M. Seckler, ed., *Handbuch der Fundamentaltheologie* (note 133), pp. 100–123, esp. pp. 117–121.

in new ways. This is so because, on the one hand, the depth of the mystery which God makes known and reveals Himself as is unfathomable. On the other hand, all attempts to formulate and pass on doctrine in faith are characterized by their limited historical nature and bear the traces of the thinking of their time. They are therefore not understandable and helpful for all time so that "in this habitual usage of the Church certain of these formulae gave way to new expressions which, proposed and approved by the Sacred Magisterium, presented more clearly or more completely the same meaning."[142] If we can indeed experience again and again "that a 'positive' development of doctrine through the mere recollection of magisterial formulations, although necessary, helps little, and that one must instead argue from the center of Christian faith in a more vivid and more original way, more in keeping with the times and more persuasively"[143], then this appeal cannot be realized other than through a "return", also of all those who teach, to the word of the gospel in Sacred Scripture, a "return" which is constantly willing to listen anew. "Therefore, like the Christian religion itself, all the preaching of the Church must be nourished and ruled by sacred Scripture." (*Dei Verbum* 21).

9.5.3 Conclusions

(239) As one result of our reflections we would jointly like to stress the need *to use the term "teaching office" in a* precise and *discriminating way*: In general ecclesial usage "teaching office" is normally understood as referring to those proclaimers of the word who are entrusted with a special public responsibility, and not to the *munus propheticum*, the "*officio* nature" of the common priesthood of all the baptized. In Protestantism these are the ordained pastors, the church-commissioned assistants, the bearers of church

---

142 Sacred Congregation for the Doctrine of the Faith, *Mysterium Ecclesiae*: Declaration in Defense of the Catholic Doctrine on the Church Against Certain Errors of the Present Day (June 24, 1973).

143 K. Lehmann, "Einleitung und Kommentar zu *Mysterium Ecclesia*," in: Kongregation für die Glaubenslehre, Erklärung "*Mysterium Ecclesiae*: Zur katholischen Lehre über die Kirche und ihre Verteidigung gegen einige Irrtümer von heute (1973)," Trier 1975, p. 72. [Lehmann's introduction and commentary are part of the German-language publication of *Mysterium Ecclesiae*.]

administrative offices and the synods. In Catholicism this refers to the college of bishops and the holder of the Petrine office, the Bishop of Rome, as well as in a participative way to all priests and the "nonordained faithful" who are active full-time in the church and granted the *missio canonica* [canonical permission] or mandate to teach[144]. At the level of the "teaching office" doctrinal decisions can be made which claim to be binding in the church – whether due to their reception by the church or with the objective of their being received by the church. The "reservation as to that binding nature," which, according to the Protestant understanding, is necessary when considering the authoritative witness of Scripture, will have to be the subject of further discussions.

(240) With respect to the linguistic usage of the Bible, it is in any case inappropriate to set proclamation and church teaching in opposition to one another in a polarizing way. For the purpose of clarifying what is meant, however, it is legitimate to understand by "*binding teaching*" not every official proclamation, but above all that way of interpretively transmitting the word of God which combines contents of the gospel in the form of a doctrine with the straightforward objective of having it received by the church community. This way of interpreting statements of religious experience by summarizing, linking, justifying and differentiating them, which is already pronounced in the Bible itself, is characteristic of the history of the transmission of faith in such forms as baptismal creeds, rules of faith, conciliar decisions and confessional texts, among others.

(241) All these forms of "binding church teaching" are marked by their integration into the tradition process of which they themselves are a part. From this point of view they are defined by a *twofold relational character* and can also only be properly understood if this is taken into consideration. On the one hand they relate to the statements of Sacred Scripture which they seek to interpret; on the other hand they always relate in a discernible way to the

---

144 The "Instruction on Some Questions Regarding Collaboration of Nonordained Faithful in Priests' Sacred Ministry" published in 1997 reinforces this position. [The English text of this Vatican Instruction can be found in *Origins* 27, issue 24 (27 November 1997) 397; 399-409].

proclamation situation of their time of origin, to its issues and disputes. Binding church teaching is thus always the attempt to make the word of God in Sacred Scripture heard in a particular period of the church in an authentic way, to interpret it, and to protect it from falsification.

(242) In conclusion we should clearly identify what in the history of our churches, albeit in a different way in each case, has brought ecclesial teaching into disrepute and caused problems with respect to the willingness of many Christians to believe: the often great *discrepancy between the correct principles and the concrete exercise of the teaching responsibility of the church*. The church's sinfulness and constant need to reform not only have a negative impact on the actual conduct of the life of all its members, but also on the fulfilment of the responsibility to communicate the gospel in an authentic way. The history of faith includes many inglorious examples of one-sided, insufficient, misleading, distorting and incorrect interpretations of Sacred Scripture by office holders. Even where correct statements were advocated, the circumstances surrounding the claim to being binding were often such that the doctrine weighed down instead of building up, choked faith instead of awakening it, and hindered the imitation of Christ instead of making it possible.

(243) All this must be dispassionately recognized as historical and ecclesiological fact. And precisely for this reason it should be stressed at the same time that the right, indeed the duty to express such criticism flows from the word of God itself, from the critical function of Sacred Scripture in the church. The word of God in Sacred Scripture also always becomes a critical criterion for the concrete way it is transmitted when, in the *testimonium spiritus sancti* experienced jointly by the faithful and in the form of withheld reception by the church community, certain procedures and statements of official church teaching, no matter how "binding" they purport to be or like to function, may possibly prove to be detrimental, obstructive, or even contradictory to the word of the gospel. It is our joint conviction that in all such cases the promised support of the Holy Spirit of God will nevertheless preserve the church in truth. It is the Holy Spirit who "infallibly" – in God's faithfulness to His promise – preserves the church-wide confession unerringly so that all believers can remain on the path of truth.

10 Epilogue: God's Spirit in God's Word

(244) In our ecumenical endeavors to find a common foundation for the teaching on the authority of Holy Scripture in the life and doctrine of the church we have known right from the beginning that the Holy Spirit is of pivotal importance. Looking back at the working phase of our Ecumenical Study Group on the topic of "understanding Scripture" we can state: This realization has become firmly fixed and clearly defined for us.

Our shared insight that Holy Scripture is God's word is based on a new recognition of the importance of the doctrine of the inspiration of Scripture and a new understanding of it. In the life of the church throughout all the centuries this doctrine has been a conviction of faith resting on spiritual experience: When dealing with Holy Scripture at the time of the early church, throughout the Middle Ages and during the Reformation, theology, liturgy and piety always started from the assumption that God's Spirit is present and efficacious in the wording of Scripture and that at the same time this Spirit enlightens the hearts and minds of the faithful so that they may understand Scripture as God's word.

(245) A deep crisis in the understanding of inspiration arose, however, in the age of the Enlightenment and through its influence in the theology and teaching of the Protestant church. The Catholic church tried to protect itself from this crisis by, among other things, emphasizing the continuity of ecclesial traditions to safeguard the authority of Scripture and by stressing the authority of the teaching office of the bishops and the pope to safeguard the truth of revelation in Scripture and tradition.

(246) The Bible Movement in the theology and piety of the 20th century as well as new theological awakenings caused both Protestants and Catholics to recognize anew the importance of the dynamic blowing of God's Spirit (cf. Jn 3:8, 4:24) in Holy Scripture and in the life of the church with Holy Scripture. The Ecumenical Movement has been inspired and fostered by this in a significant way. The fundamental teaching of the Reformation that Holy Scripture is the sole source of our knowledge of the truth of the gospel (*sola scriptura*) can also be advocated by Catholics if one means by this that Holy

Scripture "must be read and interpreted according to the same Spirit by whom it was written" (*Dei Verbum* 12) and that the study of Scripture "is, as it were, the soul of sacred theology" (*Dei Verbum* 24). On the other hand, the Catholic teaching concerning Scripture and tradition becomes acceptable to Protestants if one means by tradition the living, Spirit-filled tradition of the earliest apostolic church which acquired its written form in the books of the New Testament, was accepted by the church along with Old Testament Scripture as "canon" under the guidance of the Holy Spirit, and is interpreted and passed down in worship and teaching ever anew in dynamic proclamation.

(247) With its postulate that the "teaching office is not above the word of God, but serves it" (*Dei Verbum* 10), the Second Vatican Council established an important precondition so that a common basic view could begin to develop in ecumenical dialogues with regard to the relationship between Holy Scripture, tradition and the teaching office. Of decisive importance for this development is the agreement that the one Spirit of God, who is, as a matter of principle, always superior to the spirit of humans, is at work in Holy Scripture as well as in its interpretation.

(248) We can thus state together:

– Through the Holy Spirit Holy Scripture is *God's word* in the words of the human witnesses enlightened by Him.
– Through the Holy Spirit the triune God is present *in the worship* of His church in which Holy Scripture is read as God's word and interpreted into the life of the faithful in vivid, contemporary language.
– Through the Holy Spirit the church is able to recognize ever anew in *Jesus Christ*, who is the Word of the Father, the living *essence of the Holy Scriptures* of both testaments in the unity and diversity of their witnesses.
– Through the Holy Spirit the activity of God in *law and gospel* can be understood and experienced in the history of God's people in the old covenant and in the history of His new covenantal people.
– Through the Holy Spirit the *interpretation of Scripture* takes place *in the Liturgia* [worship], *Martyria* [witness] *and Diakonia* [service] of the

church. It is this one Spirit of God, "moving the heart" and "opening the eyes of the mind" (*Dei Verbum* 5) who "calls, gathers together, enlightens and makes holy the whole Church on earth and keeps it with Jesus in the one, true faith." (Luther, *Small Catechism*, explanation of the third article of faith).

– Through the Holy Spirit the *scholarly exegesis* of the Old and the New Testament acquires both its central criterion for understanding the biblical texts as testimonies to God's working in each particular historical period and situation and its abiding significance for the life and teaching of the church of all times.
– Through the Holy Spirit the authority of Holy Scripture as the written form of the *living apostolic tradition* of the gospel which is normative for all times is recognized in the proclamation and teaching of the church so that it is God Himself who lets the divine truth of His words in Holy Scripture and in its living proclamation glow in the hearts of the human listeners.
– Through the Holy Spirit the church as *the entire people of God* is gifted and empowered to witness to the gospel.
– Through the Holy Spirit members of the church are called, gifted, sent and empowered to be "*servants of the word*"; with this mission the *apostolic responsibility* for the correct interpretation of Scripture and the preservation of the truth of its witness in the teaching and life of the church is also entrusted to them.

(249) Thus in the interpretation of Holy Scripture, in the preservation of the teaching of the gospel, and in Christian life with the gospel the Holy Spirit of God and of Jesus Christ proves Himself to be the mover and guarantor of all binding testimony to the word of God in the midst of His people from the very beginning and throughout all the ages of the church. It is He who guides the church "into all the truth" (Jn 16:13). Every religious service, every interpretation of Holy Scripture, and every exercise of spiritual meditation on Scripture begins with the petition that He come:

"*Veni Sancte Spiritus!*"

www.ingramcontent.com/pod-product-compliance
Ingram Content Group UK Ltd.
Pitfield, Milton Keynes, MK11 3LW, UK
UKHW041923210426
5322IPUK00002B/14

9 783631 653043